THE
GOLDEN
ORACLE

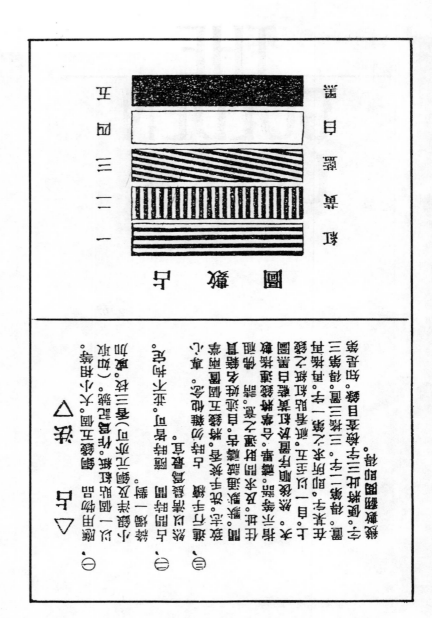

A page from *Men Li Ming Yuen Bao Zhen*

THE GOLDEN ORACLE

The Ancient Chinese Way to Prosperity

Translated by Ch'ao-Li Chi
Commentary by Khigh Dhiegh

ARCO PUBLISHING, INC.
New York

Published by Arco Publishing, Inc.
215 Park Avenue South, New York, N.Y. 10003

Library of Congress Cataloging in Publication Data

Main entry under title:
The Golden oracle.

   "A complete translation of a traditional Chinese
oracle"—Pref.
   1. Divination—China. I. Chi, Ch'ao-Li. II. Dhiegh,
Khigh. III. Title: Ancient Chinese way to prosperity.
BF1773.2.C5G64   1983   133.3   82-18471
ISBN 0-668-05661-4 (Cloth edition)
ISBN 0-668-05913-4 (Paper edition)

Printed in the United States of America

10   9   8   7   6   5   4   3   2   1

Contents

Preface

Oracles have played significant roles throughout history. They have also rendered a very meaningful service in the lives of ordinary, average human beings who participated in that same history.

This book invites you to investigate the nature of oracles and shares with you a traditional Chinese oracle. You will be given all the instructions necessary to use this Golden Oracle to become successful. When you have completed all of Part I of this book, you will be fully able to work the oracle. The phrase *work the oracle* appears in a *Penguin Dictionary of English* definition, which in part reads: ". . . work the oracle, obtain one's end by intrigue; raise money." We see that oracles are associated with monetary matters in cultural quarters other than Chinese.

The term *oracle* is frequently associated with the term *prophecy.* The difference between an oracle and a prophecy is that prophecy occurs as an act of foretelling the future through extraordinary inspiration or insight. One does not "work" a prophecy. It happens. It manifests with sudden revelation. An oracle literally has to be "worked." A prescribed technique (ritual) sets the process into action of interrelating a selected concern of an individualized consciousness, a time, a location, a ceremonial exercise, and an oracle response, culminating as an experience describable as subjectively satisfying.

We do not claim this Golden Oracle to be a magical device of supernatural potential or capability. To the contrary, we shall exert every effort to bring you to understand how it and almost any other oracle are susceptible to natural explanations. The nature of oracles seems to us to be a compound of cosmic processes, flowing intelligence, and psychological-emotional resonances. We suggest that most oracles manifest as instances of voluntary intuition.

Intuition, like our neurological system, functions dualistically, through voluntary and involuntary expression. Involuntary intuition registers as "a feeling," "a hunch," "a sudden urge." Voluntary intuition—like voluntary neurophysiologic selectives—performs under controlled, intentional direction for a purposed objective.

There have been many articles and books written about intuition, describing it in many ways. The explanation encouraged here is that intuition becomes the art or science of recognizing. When one works an oracle, the effort made aims to find a means to relax, so that one may flow harmoniously with the cosmic currents of intelligence and energy, resulting in one's insight becoming penetrative. With this heightened perception, one continues executing plans to complete important projects designed to enrich one's life.

Intuition implies universality. Every person and every creature behaves preeminently as an intuitive organism at birth. Nonhuman creatures continue making use of intuitive faculties to a much greater degree and for a much longer time than do humans. Indeed, the human use of intuition very quickly lessens with maturation and is discouraged by our mechanical, technical, and cybernetic culture. Intuition soon becomes an insignificant part of our daily experience. It's given little or no thought by most of us except, perhaps, when we are anxiously involved in a situation of suspenseful uncertainty. For many, the immediate understanding of intuition proves to be distant and hazy. Let us remedy this situation by referring to *Webster's*, where we read, "intuition: the direct perception of truths, facts, etc., independent of any reasoning process. *Phil.:* The immediate cognition of an object not inferred or determined by a previous cognition of the same object. Pure, untaught, noninferential knowledge."

At the moment of emergence (be it through birth, hatching,

larval metamorphosis, or other process), every creature acti-vates immediately in an untaught behavior pattern. Each or-ganism automatically self-initiates and/or responds to some natural parental prodding, so that it performs in a manner that ensures its continuance. No one sends a newborn to pre-nipple school to teach it how to suckle at its mother's breast. A baby intuitively knows (independently of any reasoning process) what to do. Involuntary intuition initiates all postnatal survival me-chanics. Life continuity processes are basically mundanely nat-ural but are inexplicable marvels, nevertheless.

This book introduces a Chinese oracle tradition still prac-ticed, with complete instructions on how to use the Golden Oracle to successfully prosper in the selected areas of your desires. In Chapter 5, "The Development of Oracles," you will find anecdotes that illustrate a variety of purposes and ways in which this Golden Oracle functions as a guide to prosperity. The examples will be useful to anyone wishing to analyze the energy vibration of anticipated projects. In this way you can determine how and when to act for each selected concern and the best course of action or nonaction to take.

In Part II of this book, you will find a complete translation of a traditional Chinese oracle, with appended commentaries and copious explanations. Part I constitutes a formulary of the-ories, philosophies, and psychological evaluations concerning oracles in general. In this way, we have tried to prepare a book of value to both the metaphysical dilettante and the more deeply curious pursuer.

In this book, you will find various ways by which you can develop your ability to make practical use of this and other oracles. You will be informed of their historical origin and made familiar with the different kinds of oracles and the purposes for which they are worked.

Can you invent your own oracle? That question will be examined in these pages. Can a person be an oracle? Do oracles involve us in religious or antireligious practices and beliefs? How are oracles made? Are oracles reliable? Which oracle ex-tant today has the greatest antiquity? Are there similarities between oracle guidance and psychological counseling? Can oracles be useful in business? Can consulting oracles make you insane? Do oracles appeal only to the uneducated? These and many other questions will be considered in the pages that follow.

As you begin reading this book, you may find some of the phrasing awkward. This experience results from the *is* of identity being absent from certain chapters and portions of this exposition.

Since precision of understanding lessens because of "confusion through the lack of discrimination between the 'is' of identity . . . and the 'is' of predication, the 'is' of existence, and the 'is' used as an auxiliary verb, I have tried to eliminate most of the *is*'s from those particular sections. *Is*, in all its guises, appears throughout most of the text. It has been excluded from portions of this Preface, Chapter 1, "The Science Behind the Art of Oracles," and Chapter 4, "Chance, Cycles, and Synchronicity." And I suspect that even this minimal effort must delight the spirit of the American poet-philosopher George Santayana. It was his observation that the *is* of identity innocently marries different things, even though no two things are identical. In one of his writings, *Skepticism and Animal Faith*, he wrote: "Whenever I use the word *is*, except for sheer tautology, I deeply misuse it; and when I discover my error, the world seems to fall asunder and the members of my family no longer know one another."[1]

Working oracles can be very enjoyable. The study of oracles can help in heightening your intuitive senses. As you develop "oracle consciousness," you will become more alert and experience a new excitement that comes with being able to anticipate the expected and the unexpected. This book will serve to guide you so that you will be able to select your own route through the oracular seas and arrive safely and satisfactorily at the port you have determined upon.

Set sail and voyage upon the oracle oceans of tradition. Rev the engines and fly through the oracle skies of present consciousness. Launch the rockets and pierce the oracle space of an innovative tomorrow. Be happy, be protected, be conse-

[1]Alfred Korzybski: *Science and Sanity*, International Non-Aristotelian Library Publishing, Co.: Connecticut, 1973.

crated. As you develop this interest you will be able to opt what voltage of cosmic charge you want. Grow in electric consciousness and become a source of inspiration to all you encounter.

ḞU = Happiness, luck, blessing
FǓ = To feed, to nourish
FÙ = Rich, abundant, wealth

May you be blessed with happiness and luck, so that you will be able to nourish many, because of your riches and great wealth.

—KHIGH DHIEGH

Foreword

When Dr. Dhiegh asked me to write the foreword to this book on the Golden Oracle, I could not help but wonder if there was anything similar in my own tradition. To my surprise, there did exist such instruments. The Urim and Thummin. Urim and Thummmim are words variously translated "revelation and truth," or "those whose words give light and are fulfilled." They were sacred instruments used by the priests of Yahweh to obtain guidance from God on important issues. The oracle, as mentioned in Numbers 27:12 and I Samuel 14:41-42, was designed to indicate which of two alternative statements was correct. It is important to note here that, although a priest was needed to use the oracle, he employed no special technique of interpretation as did the diviners of other religions, or as did the Golden Oracle itself.

The Golden Oracle, as explained by Dr. Dhiegh, seems to be completely opposite the Urim. First, Dr. Dhiegh maintains that the Golden Oracle, or any oracle, is not used to facilitate communications with some personal preternatural force, be that force divine or demonic. This is important for me. Someone in the Judeo-Christian-Islamic tradition would find it "ungodly" to consult any other preternatural personal force than God for direction in life. Dr. Dhiegh has instead anchored the reality of all oracles within the reality of the Dao.* The Dao is the unifying principle that underlies the universe. I can best understand the Dao through the Jungian concept of synchronicity. Psychiatrist Jean Bolen has stated the following.

Through synchronicity the Western mind may come to

*Dao is the new official approved "Pinyin" transliteration for "Tao."

know what the Tao is. As a concept, synchronicity bridges East and West, philosophy and psychology, right brain and left. Synchronicity is the Tao of Psychology, relating the individual to the totality. If we personally realize that synchronicity is at work in our lives, we feel connected, rather than isolated and estranged from others; we feel ourselves part of a divine, dynamic, interrelated universe.**

Perhaps this has been one of the more significant effects of the Golden Oracle upon my life: what Dr. Dhiegh has referred to as "oracle consciousness." In dealing with the Golden Oracle, I have become more sensitized to the occurrence of synchronistic events in my life. Hence, I have been forced to examine these synchronistic events of my life as though they were symbols in a dream offering to me insights into myself and insights into the basic interconnectedness of all reality.

The second manner in which the Golden Oracle differs from the Urim and Thummim is in the manner of manipulation. The Urim, from all available indications, expressed divine revelation to the priest by the shining or dullness of the stones of his breastplate, due to some virtue inherent in them. The Golden Oracle, however, must be interpreted from a text. Obviously, the Golden Oracle is filled with a large amount of material that springs from the particular social, ecological, historical, religious, economic, political life-situation of the ancient author(s). Now the question arises, "Is it possible for a Western Christian, like me, to experience the depth of understanding of the wisdom of the Golden Oracle as would an Eastern Buddhist?" To fully enter into the Golden Oracle, or any other ancient text, we need to transpose our understanding from the present (with our presuppositions and prejudices) to a different space and time (with their own presuppositions and prejudices). Furthermore, after having entered into the understanding of that time we must again spring forward into our own time and retransform that understanding into the symbols with which we are most comfortable. There are two kinds of symbols with which we must work. The first and simpler of

**The Tao of psychology-Jean Shinoda Bolen, M.D.-Harper & Row, Publishers-1979 p. 7

these two groups is the group of archetypal symbols that emerge from our collective unconscious. These symbols sometimes change from one culture to another, but the basic hopes and fears manifested in the symbols seem to be constant. Hence even though the dragon, for example, is the symbol of good in one culture and the symbol of evil in another, I have always been reasonably able to translate and to react to these symbols in the way I believe the ancient author intended, once I understood his cultural view.

The more challenging undertaking for me has been in the second group of symbols — the personal and culturally-reinforced symbols that have, for the most part, gone unexamined in my life. I do not imply that these symbols are either constructive or destructive, only unexamined and at times, even unknown. I have mostly experienced this process of discovering unknown personal presuppositions through Hebrew and Christian scriptures. In trying to understand the meaning of a particular passage, I have tried to place myself in the place of the ancient author. I must presuppose a different cosmology, as well as many other perceptions of reality arising from the author's particular social, ecological, historical, religious, economic, political life-situation. Often, just trying to do this makes me aware of aspects of my perception of reality that are colored by unexamined presuppositions.

In dealing with Dr. Dhiegh's explanation of the Golden Oracle, two further presuppositions came to be examined. First, there is my presupposition that there exists an absolute time and an absolute coordinate system through which events could be judged as occurring before, after, or simultaneous to another event. The English language further encourages this presupposition through its use of tense. Contrary to this presupposition stands the special and general theory of relativity. Similarly, I had not previously examined my presupposition that events occur in the form of cause and effect. Contrary to that stands the theory of Quantum physics.

Though these two presuppositions came to my attention while reading the commentary section to the Golden Oracle, other presuppositions were discovered in the reading of the text and others yet to emerge. Here, the Western reader must assume the responsibility of opening himself/herself to the growth-producing challenges of understanding old views through Western categories. The portion of this challenge that is most difficult is the religious challenge. Here we are usually most reluctant to give up some of our views; indeed, some are in fact impossible because of our religious commitment.

This imminence can also be seen in the last difference between the Golden Oracle and the Urim. The Urim and Thummim required the priest to be used whereas, the Golden Oracle can be used by anyone. Here the quality and depth of relationship manifest themselves. Where the Urim and Thummim concentrated on the relationship with God (as symbolized in the priest), the Golden Oracle concentrates on the relationship with oneself. The presupposition here is that everyone affects reality; the principle of synchronicity is applicable to everyone. Within myself I have noticed that, as my relationship with myself developed, so did my relationship with my God, and vice versa. Both relationships seem to be complementing sides of the same coin.

Whether Dr. Dhiegh's presentation coincides with your or my view of reality is not at issue. What is at issue is that his presentation as well as the Golden Oracle can help us increase our awareness of ourselves both as individuals and as members or fibers within the cosmic reality.

Dr. Dhiegh is fond of telling me that he "only shares his prejudices," for he might change his view totally by tomorrow. He never proselytizes, he only shares to enrich. If we accept this view then truly our consciousness has been elevated through the sharing of ideas.

—Father John Giandelone

Part I

Playful divining no benefit.
Sincere seeking then effective.
As echo following sound,
As shadow accompanying form;
Good man becomes rich,
Bright virtue leaves fragrance.

Translated from
Men Li Ming Yuen Bao Zhen

CHAPTER 1

The Science Behind the Art of Oracles

You will discover that this book expounds sense and nonsense. Its pages will reflect wisdom and the absence of it. In order to share the perspective and understand the theme of this book, it may be necessary to make some adjustments in your accustomed usage and interpretation of language. You may have to modify your concepts of the nature of "reality" along with the role of causality in your day-to-day living. These pages introduce for your use an established oracle—an oracle that has become traditional among many Chinese, who turn to it when they are seeking guidance in becoming prosperous. Along with this presentation, you are being invited to examine the concept of this and other oracles, to determine how coherently an oracle can function in an environment of modern scientific understanding, in which society prides itself on being primarily concerned with a scientific orientation to existence.

One may challenge the implication inherent in the title of this chapter. We are not insisting that a science irrefutably underlies oracles. Rather, we are inviting you to investigate the history of oracles by examining this Golden Oracle. In this way, you may determine what factual statements, if any, can be made about oracles, and you may also test the degree of probability of correctness of any inferential statements implied by the oracle.

What does it mean to say one knows the science of an oracle? The word *science*, as used in our language, communicates the nonverbal experience in consciousness of knowing. *To know* insinuates definiteness of perception and thought. It is largely determined by the way we think. This leads us to observe that experience and knowledge are polarized aspects of a single event. The event itself is best expressed in the hyphenated form; *experience-knowledge*, emphasizing that both terms are inseparable aspects of a single phenomenon. Thus the science behind oracles can only be discovered through experientially working an oracle.

The oracle included in this book represents only one of innumerable systems utilizing symbols for activating intuitive insight and analytical perceptiveness in human beings. From immemorial times, people have turned to similar devices whenever they experience uncertainty and apprehensiveness concerning particular matters in which they come to be involved.

Many of these parapsychological systems (tarot, *I Ching*, numerology, astrology, palmistry, spiritualism, and so on) hold a charismatic fascination for those who have faith in them. Not so for those who need to understand before they can believe. Included in this text are explanations, descriptions, and examples of a scientific, evidential nature (some may regard the use of this material as quasi scientific) that, it is hoped, will persuade you to acknowledge the possibility that this oracle (and other systems of symbolic images serving as metaphorical indicators) can have a pragmatic function.

In this book, quotations from a variety of scholarly, historical, and scientific sources will be introduced to support and stand as possible explanations of the phenomenal forces at play in the metaphysical world. As you come to flow with the ideas expressed, keep in mind that the interpretations given and the understandings concluded are not necessarily shared or endorsed by the distinguished originators of the thoughts, statements, or research findings quoted.

We ask you to recognize that the interpretations expressed herein are as valid and honest as any others. After all, who can subjectively know how a flavor excites another's taste buds? Who can determine what vibration frequency a color has to the eye of a color-blind individual? Any rational conclusion must hold that in some instances, individual responses and interpretations may not correspond with the majority or with the average. Yet in all instances, the nature of that experienced by the individual remains exactly what he or she experiences.

This being so, both physics and metaphysics should be recognized as approaches of inquiry and perspective concerned with the natural. They are disciplines concerned with seeking and interpreting matter, ideas, and experiences that are both average and outside the average. All things and experiences that are average and outside the average make up the natural. That conviction stands as one of the fundamental premises of this book. All that exists must be natural!

The skeletal structure of our thesis holds: given all of the specific ingredients, influences, genetic composition, time, space, and manifested physicality, that which exists cannot be other than its existence. Therefore it is natural. That which differs from the norm may be atypical, grossly unusual, outside the average, and so forth, but it remains, nevertheless, natural.

If the physicist Dr. Fritjof Capra proves to be correct in suggesting that "basic structures of the material world are determined, ultimately, by the way in which we look at this world. In other words, the observed patterns of matter are nothing but reflections of patterns of mind," then it follows that all momentarily nonaverage things, conditions, and/or persons, may be—in one place or another, at one time or another, individually or collectively—average. In other words, all things are desirable or undesirable, according to the consensus at a given time. In fact, Capra's assertion can be seen as a modern reiteration of the biblical declaration "In the beginning was the word" (logos), the thought, and without thought, not anything was made that was made.[2]

If humanity could realize and accept as fact the potency of thought, people could coexist individually and collectively in a flowing, ordinating harmony. And this would be irrespective of whether the concept has acceptance and understanding academically or not.

Every effort to enforce a person-created definition of law

[2]Fritjof Capra, Ph.D.: "Quark Physics Without Quarks," *The American Journal of Physics*, January 1979.

as an absolute, eventually terminates in traumatic experiences having disastrous consequences. Most human beings tend to ignore that the opacity of human comprehension disables us, so that we cannot recognize or accept the infinite kinds of forces and influences that affect us.

Only a few creatures can see the wind. But all can see the effects of wind. Are there any who can see electricity? But all can see the effects of electricity. Only a few can see or read thoughts. But all can see the effects of thought. And while few can see thoughts, we all think! Every thought transforms into some kind of seeing within the consciousness of the thinker. Suggesting the color red with the printed word *red* immediately initiates a process of transformations:

The printed word *red*, registering on the eye, communicates through vibrations of neurological impulses the perception of the black-inked word *red*. This registers upon appropriate organic brain centers that create from the printed (in black) word *red* the consciousness of the color red, carrying with it the summation that averages out all of one's previous experiences of the color red.

Perhaps the most amazing thing about all of this comes with the realization that each individual's experience of red will be unique.

We live in a universe comprised of infinite instances, each one being unique. There may be closely approximating matchings, so-called replicas of a thing or an event, appraised as identical. However, there can be no precisely absolute multiple-sameness. The concept of multiple-sameness (often carelessly taken to be implied by the term *identical*) misleads. A phrase spoken two or more times may be mistaken to be duplicated, or to be manifesting multiple-sameness, because of the fact that it has been repeated. In a similar way, anything duplicated may be mistaken as an instance of multiple-sameness. But in the most highly refined understanding of sameness, there can be only one thing the same: the thing itself. All other similarities are identifiable through comparison, which expresses the meaning of "identical."

The purpose of this seeming digression is to throw light upon one aspect of the nature of oracles. The Golden Oracle consists of 125 responses. Each response is divided into an explanation and a judgment. To the curious mind comes the question: "How can 125 responses be directly meaningful to the countless millions of instances it will be called upon to relate to?"

The perplexity exemplified here comes from giving primary importance to words, while ignoring each experienced consultation as a unique actuality of an individualized consciousness. In the actual process of living, experience comes first, and the descriptives of language follow—a fact that seems to evade us, because we are trapped in a culture where words and language, beginning with our earliest training, are inculcated first, and it is expected that the experience will fit the vocabulated mold. This inversion of values should be recognized as a pathological reversal of the natural order. When we develop skill in focusing first upon the experience, then verbalizing it, we will begin to understand how this oracle, as others, functions.

Admittedly, oracles are difficult to appraise with an open mind, especially in an environment dominantly influenced by the philosophy "get by the best you can, so long as you succeed." The kind of success here alluded to focuses on maintaining the maximum conformity compatible with acceptance. For this reason, many (if not most) people in highly evolved technological societies regard oracles as belonging in the province of charlatans and dupes. Yet fortunetelling, spiritualism, psychic investment counseling, and the selling of prayer candles and occult paraphernalia continue to be economically rewarding enterprises.

The purpose of preparing this book is to encourage the ambitious, questing after knowledge, to act with aggressive curiosity and intelligent questioning and to visualize new possibilities of understanding, which can broaden comprehension of the nature of oracles.

As with everything, workers of oracles are polarizable. They are generally recognized as ranging from "positive"—responsible, self-assured, and self-expressive persons, to "negative"—

panic-ridden, neurotic, hyperanxious individuals. Those who come closer to the positive pole work oracles as modes for extending the reach of their consciousness. Those who fall toward the negative pole work oracles as if they were magical devices for bringing them deliverance. The first type act as responsible, self-assertive persons. The latter react as whining, self-negating, hopeless creatures.

We need to state a very pertinent point to commence with: every generalization relating to oracles has limitations. Because it helps to define part of the ideological basis of this study of oracles, we will editorially paraphrase portions of a paragraph from Dr. Harry L. Weinberg's book, *Levels of Knowing and Existence.*

He noted that at this present time, it seems that people have gone from the one extreme of complete acceptance of traditional ethical, moral, and religious doctrines to the other extreme of total cultural relativism. The common conviction seems to be that all evaluative judgments considered good and valuable in one society may be judged bad and useless in another. Because of this, many people are unable to structure a substantial and meaningful ethical code for themselves. Then, Weinberg explains: "For if these codes are relative to societies, they are also relative to parts of societies and to smaller parts of these, and they must necessarily vary with the date. Consequently, it becomes almost impossible to make moral and ethical decisions with any degree of certainty and security. One result, then, is a slavish dependence on the majority opinion of the group within which they function. In short, having lost or never having found standards of their own, individuals become what has been called 'outer-directed men'—the hollow men swaying in the winds of ethical fashions, clinging to the group for a security bought at the price of intellectual freedom and self-actualization." We suggest that in working an oracle for a situation, one is, psychologically, seeking to find a standard of one's own—at least, in the related instance.[3]

When a person turns to working an oracle for reaching a decision, it may be, in part, a substitutive act, compensating

[3]Harry L. Weinberg Ph.D.: *Levels of Knowing and Existence,* Institute of General Semantics: Connecticut, 1973.

for hesitating to perpetrate a moral or ethical action with conviction and certitude. When recourse to an oracle is exercised as a freely elected option, it could indicate an intentional desire to amplify one's intuitive insights into the matter being addressed. However, if one turns to working an oracle because one is bewildered and lacks even the haziest idea or feeling of how to deal with the matter at hand, one is most apt to misread and misinterpret the oracle's response. For then it is no longer an act of determination, but one of desperation.

In order to work an oracle productively, one's self-image must include an awareness of its wholeness and connectivity with everything surrounding oneself. The new physics suggests that all materialities interact at subtle and ephemeral energy levels. Being aware of this helps one avoid becoming a lost, "outer-directed" person, clinging to group mores rather than structuring one's own ethical code.

No oracle is manipulatable so as to eliminate all difficulties, all anxieties, or all worries. No oracle will respond satisfyingly to every complexity that troubles us. An oracle must first be recognized as only a small part of a process that enables us to control selected internal and external environments of our experiences.

We become experienced in two ways: through involvement by intentional design, and through involvement by happenstance. The latter experience occurs involuntarily, without intention or preparation. It may be expected or unexpected. Also, it may sometimes be sudden and sometimes not. All happenstance experiences can only be identified retrospectively, and most likely will be associated with good-luck or bad-luck omens rather than with scripted oracles. Involvement by voluntary design may be described as learned or learnable experience. The Golden Oracle, when worked as a metaphysical device, becomes a participating element of learnable experiences. Good-luck pieces we prejudicially classify with happenstance experiences do not involve the active exercise of will or thought. One wears them, carries them, or just has them around. The belief (unexplored inference) holds that they bring joyous good fortune. Oracles such as the *I Ching* and the Golden Oracle involve the operator in various kinds and degrees of ritual, mental and emotional preparation (psychological conditioning), and intellectual and literary responsivity. With a good-luck charm, one can quickly lose awareness of its presence. How often many of us have heard someone lament, "Oh no! I've lost my good-luck piece." The oracle, deliberately selected and acted upon, immediately becomes a part of a planned and learnable experience.

I would like to share a personal experience with you that illustrates the working of the Golden Oracle.

In 1979, just after the translation of the Chinese text of this book was completed and the individual commentaries were added to each of the 125 responses, we were eager to find a publisher. After we sent the manuscript to a publisher (*not* the actual publisher of this book), we complied with all the traditional ceremonial observances and manipulated the five coins three times, resulting in the color symbol for number 66: Blue, White, Blue, classified "Low and Low."

We were greatly surprised and very disappointed. To work the oracle means to read it, reread it, then think upon it. You must seek to "feel" the meaning and guidance metaphorically communicated. Below is the oracle response followed by our interpretation.

EXPLANATION: You are given one White between two Blues. Metal overcomes wood backward and forward. No freedom to move in either direction. The image is snow filling up the pass. It will be necessary to wait till the spring, when wood flourishes again, before there can be a turn of fortune.

JUDGMENT: The fates are blocked. Wealth hopeless. No way to go forward. No one will pity you. To venture out will bring many calamities. Better return and wait out the time before greater losses are encountered.

COMMENTARY: The conditions which presently surround you are greatly restrictive. There is not much choice or opportunity for self-expression or elective determination. "To wait till spring, when wood flourishes again" means biding one's time until the fixed and frozen conditions of the present thaw out and an elasticity of new ideas and permissiveness allows for the development of new techniques to achieve goals of desirability and fortuitous destiny.

INTERPRETATION: The manuscript had already been mailed. It was too late to revise it before the publisher would make a final decision about it. This was our understanding of the phrase "No freedom to move in either direction." We decided to resign ourselves to the probability that the manuscript would be rejected. Three weeks later our expectations were fulfilled by the return of our manuscript.
Our first positive thought, after digesting the sad confirmation of the oracle's response, was that we should revise the manuscript.

We reviewed our work meticulously, correcting and improving it in every way we could. We were determined to be ready to resubmit it the following spring. But as we kept studying the oracle response, we sensed the feeling that spring didn't necessarily refer to the next vernal equinox, rather, that the phrase "when wood flourishes again" implied a longer wait. For the sapling to grow so that it may produce seeds and flourish, it needs more than one round of seasons.

As it turned out, our subsequent interpretation was correct. The word *spring* figured literally in finally signing a contract with our present publisher. This signing took place in the spring of 1982.

At this point I decided to work again the Golden Oracle for a response to this question: "Will the publication of *The Golden Oracle* be successful?"

On this occasion I had gone to the Shrine of Infinite Inspiration at the Inner Truth Looking Place (Zhong Fu Guan) Daoist Sanctuary. I read the *I Ching* text for the day from the *Daoist Book of Days,* and recited the general focusing thought.

With this awakening,
I look inward and outward,
Knowing the day is well-come.
In this day I shall experience Dao,
Fulfilling my expectations.

Then I settled myself at the oracle table and manipulated the coins, which resulted in the Golden Oracle response number 41: Yellow, White, Yellow, classified "Up and Up."

EXPLANATION: White between two Yellows. This cast pictures earth producing metal with more production promised. The image is gold in the earth. Great profit. One will chance upon guidance. No laborious search necessary.

JUDGMENT: Wealth and fortune certain. The time of discovery has arrived. Someone will point out the location. Great profit. A chance meeting will be most fortunate.

COMMENTARY: The likelihood is very great that you will be approached by someone with an offer that will be very advantageous to you. Pointing out the location refers not exclusively to a geographical spot, but also to the area of pursuit wherein great advance and profit await you.

INTERPRETATION: Aside from being pleased and stimulated by the response, I felt it was significant that the word *chance* appeared twice in the text of the response. After all, the matter brought to the oracle was the oracle itself. And what other identification can we give an oracle, if not that of being a construct of and for chance?

"Earth producing metal with more production promised." Accepting that earth is a metaphor for the process of responsive sensitivity, I interpreted this phrase as meaning that I had been using my awareness responsively to particular vibrations of intelligence. This resulted in this book, and as I continue to keep in this vibration of cosmic flow, more production will be rewarded me. And the phrase "One will chance upon guidance" seemed a confirmation of what has been a continuing experience throughout my life. Accidentally chancing upon information, discovery, relationships, opportunities, and so forth enables me to progress and develop in a desired way at a selected time. The Judgment and Commentary texts seemed to me, in this instance, reinforcements of what was expressed in the Explanation.

These two workings of the Golden Oracle illustrate what the title of this chapter hints at. Oracles are artistic activators of scientific forces. Oracles are an art form. They are imaginative and present a special example for each instance of application. Art conscientiously strives to communicate subjective qualities of response to aesthetic abstractions like beauty and harmony. Oracles parallel this by expressing themselves as personal responses to psychological and physiological abstractions like anxiety and fear. Artists turn to their media as they are excited by aesthetic stimuli. Questing individuals turn to oracles as they become intensely concerned about an anxiety or fear. Through the working of oracles, the human spirit moves to intuit the mysteries of nature.

To mention the mystical does not contradict science, even though it holds "that reason is the only medium for understanding." And as Dr. R. G. H. Siu notes: "There may be other wellsprings of enlightenment. . . . But to judge something that lies beyond reason by means of reason itself does not appear reasonable. . . . After all, scientists are a mite superstitious themselves, if we care to put the proposition thus. They *do* believe in baffling unknowns; they *do* have faith in the existence of things beyond the compass of their current knowledge. Otherwise where do their research problems originate and why is the unknown pursued so vigorously?"[4]

Most everyone will concede that rational knowledge and rationalized procedures dominate the routine activities of the majority of scientific projects. But never entirely. Somewhere along the line, if one investigates thoroughly enough, one finds that the most antiseptically rigid and mathematically precise scientific attainment has been complemented by intuition. Intuition resembles shape—a very factual thing, readily cognized in our understanding. But one can no more describe the intu-

[4]R.G.H. Siu Ph.D.: *The Tao of Science*, M.I.T. Press: Massachusetts, 1957.

ition of intuition than one can tell another anything about the shape of shape.

When we seek to verify the existence or nonexistence of a science behind the art of oracles, all progress will be determined by our ability to recognize the multiple uses of abstractions. To most persons, oracles appear to be constructs of mystifying, ambiguous abstractions, devoid of clarity. Nevertheless, the concepts and symbols constituting the structure of any oracle, when creatively interpreted, enable us to cope with the actuality holding our interest. An oracle system can be regarded as a map of cosmic consciousness. Now, different travelers will select different maps and yet successfully arrive at a common destination. Likewise, people having common concerns, seeking a single goal, can and will choose different oracles and be equally fulfilled.

The language of an oracle, often very elastic, lacks precision. The individual words and separate phrases usually have several alternate meanings. Certain indications may escape one's attention on a conscious level. For this reason, maximum relaxation and holding a beta level are most conducive to experiencing the most meaning from an oracle response.

Recall from our examples cited earlier how the report of the first working of the oracle in connection with the publication of this book indicated that a degree of anxiety initiated the decision to consult the oracle. In this instance, the anxiety had overtones of a low-key kind of desperation and a moderated eagerness. In the second working of the oracle related to this book, the nature of the anxiety differed. In this case, excitement and hopeful anticipation with vibrations of positive expectation highlighted the anxiety. In short, the second use of the oracle was prompted by my being in a receptive mood, wanting to be inspired.

Most decisions to work an oracle are induced by a reaction to some kind of anxiety or fear. The practical effectiveness and productive culmination of oracle experiences increase with the insightful deepening of subjective interpretation. If these considerations are meaningful, then oracles may be adjudged as being both an art form and a science.

CHAPTER 2

Philosophical Speculations Concerning Oracles

The acceptance of oracles as scientifically sound modalities seems a very likely promise of quantum physics. We are blessed with scientist-seers such as J. S. Bell, John Clausner, Stuart Freedman, Jack Sarfatti, and Henry Pierce Stapp, plus prophet-philosophers like David Bohm, Alfred Korzybski, R. G. H. Siu, Henry L. Weinberg, and Alfred North Whitehead, who are introducing humanity to a startlingly new understanding of its nature and its potential function as an inseparable part of an "unbroken wholeness," or to use Bohm's other term, "that-which-is." Modern science discloses that the actuality of our life consciousness and our environment differs drastically from our heretofore traditional ways of conceptualizing it.

An old metaphysical teaching, traceable to Hindu thought, was that of all things being "this and that" or "this and not-this." The teaching continued, oblivious to the consternation and scorning rejection of scientists, who, not too long ago, taught that "this is this" and "that is that" and they exist separately. Today, many of the same scientists enlighten us with their latest discovery: "this" and "that" are not separate entities, but different forms of the same thing. To make the matter better understood, let us turn to Gary Zukov's *The Dancing Wu Li Masters:*

In 1964, J. S. Bell, a physicist at the European Organization for Nuclear Research (CERN) in Switzerland, zeroed in on

this strange connectedness in a manner that may make it the central focus of physics in the future. Dr. Bell published a mathematical proof which . . . theorem was reworked and refined over the following ten years until it emerged in its present form.

Bell's theorem is a mathematical construct which, as such, is indecipherable to the nonmathematician. Its implications, however, could affect profoundly our basic world view. Some physicists are convinced that it is the most important single work, perhaps, in the history of physics. One of the implications of Bell's theorem is that, at a deep and fundamental level, the "separate parts" of the universe are connected in an intimate and immediate way.

In short, Bell's theorem and the enlightened experience of unity are very compatible.

We prophesy that we are at the threshold of a time when humankind will again take oracles seriously, recognizing that they are capable of materializing an awareness of the potentials being structured by the energies and mystery of our desires, intentions, and visualizations. Already, persons familiar with modern scientific research are exhibiting a less snide attitude toward reported instances of paranormal phenomena. Take note of the following quotation, also from *The Dancing Wu Li Masters:*

Superluminal quantum connectedness seems to be, on the surface at least, a possible explanation for some types of psychic phenomena. Telepathy, for example, often appears to happen instantaneously, if not faster. Psychic phenomena have been held in disdain by physicists since the days of Newton. In fact, most physicists do not even believe that they exist.

In this sense, Bell's theorem could be the Trojan horse in the physicists' camp: first, because it proves that quantum theory requires connections that appear to resemble telepathic communication, and second, because it provides the mathematical framework through which serious physicists (all physicists are serious) could find themselves discussing

types of phenomena which, ironically, they do not believe exist.[5]

Use this Golden Oracle with the knowledge that as you act in accord with the principles now being discovered, which are structuring the explanations of tomorrow, you are influencing, shaping, and experiencing the life-consciousness before you.

[5]Gary Zukov: *The Dancing Wu Li Masters,* William Morrow & Company: New York, 1979.

CHAPTER 3

Oracle Language and Symbols

Out of necessity, oracles are expressed through language and symbols. The language may be written or oral. The symbols may appear as static design or as movement. One may speculate that oracles emerged as humankind began to experience the fragmentation of its essence. At some time in a remote primordial age, a single language may have been commonly shared by all humanity. There was no need for oracles in that era. It was a time of "isness," when the divine rhetoric "I am that I am" was chorused by every human being as spontaneously as fish swim in water and birds wing through the sky. The cosmic isness was every creature's isness. The unity contained the isness of the cat sleeping in a comfortable chair along with the isness of a drifting cloud in the outside sky. Oracles had to come into being after humankind lost its isness consciousness, that is, after humankind left the garden of innocence and became engrossed in the business of thinking, choosing, deciding, acquiring knowledge, and arrogating responsibility—in brief, after humankind awakened to and acted upon the desire for freedom. The desire for freedom led to the yearning for separation—the yearning of human intelligence to alchemically transmute its nature as an *individualized component within* the cosmic pattern, into that of being an *individual exponent of* the cosmic pattern. Once separation was accomplished, humanity discovered that it did not ensure independent happiness, and that freedom was a relative thing. Actual freedom can never again be taken hold of until humanity returns to the abode it so deliberately, though inadvertently, quitted. The use of oracles has, for thousands of years, bridged the separation of humanity's self-imposed individualism from its cosmically ordained place as part of the whole.

Proficiency in understanding and interpreting oracle pronouncements can be impeded. Difficulties arise when symbols closely resemble one another. They activate our emotions which autonomically respond in the manner that they have been culturally programmed to do. For example, snakes, mice, and bats will generally elicit negative feedback from persons bred in Western cultures. A comparable positive response could be gleaned from persons influenced by the mores of certain Eastern cultures. Remember, humankind is no longer aware that it exists as an individualized consciousness; instead, people presume themselves to be, each one, an individual and separate consciousness. But ritual observances accompanying oracles can return us to a state of isness. Through working the oracle, we each can become like unto the gods whose wisdom encompasseth all things.

To sharpen one's ability to interpret oracles, one needs to seek and practice ways of understanding the symbol-ing of language and the language-ing of symbols. Through the working of oracles, humanity spans the self-created chasm of cosmic alienation, so that once again cosmically merged, the human voice can chorus "I am that I am," and the human spirit can be aware that whatever affects one part of the organism affects all of it.

Language and symbols are indispensable to oracle pronouncements. Also, the anxiety or fear brought to the oracle, whereby it becomes purposive, can be expressed only through the use of language and symbols. Such being the fact, it behooves us to lend much attention to how a matter addressed to an oracle should be linguistically structured. Every phrase of language, in any language, contains inherent presuppositions. If there should be an error implied in the presuppositions of the phrasing or a lack of clarity, the matter of concern has not been correctly presented. It then follows that the oracle response will exhibit deficiencies in its practical meaningfulness. This requires, on the part of the consultee, a reexamination of the situation and phrasing being put to the oracle. The situation must be viewed with a fresh concern as to its appropriateness. This means that we shall have to enlarge our input of knowledgeableness about words, language, symbols, and metaphors. Let me call your attention to the close parallel between correctly structuring the matter being presented to an oracle and the need for formulating accurate information to a computer. In each case, in order for either to respond efficiently and with meaning, a relatively high degree of exactness is essential. A fascinating excitement charges through one as one observes that the need for precision in supplicating an oracle device in order to get meaningful guidance and solutions for spiritual, emotional, and psychological problems is closely akin to the preciseness demanded in using a modern electronic computer to solve our materialistic problems. This observation leads me to suggest that we may experience an increase in wisdom and a deepening of insight with working oracles by consulting the works of semanticist Dr. Harry L. Weinberg and philosopher-scientist Dr. R. G. H. Siu.

The British poet-novelist Rudyard Kipling, with intuitive perceptiveness, gave expression to one of the most fundamental facts of all ages, with the following statement: "Words are, of course, the most powerful drug used by mankind." We shall touch upon the importance of semantic research, invention, and development again and again. The importance of semantics cannot be overstressed.

It has been hinted that an oracle experience can bridge the gap between cosmic inclusion and exclusion. It has been written that "there is a time and season for every purpose under heaven." With the dawning of the Aquarian age, the time and season for oracles has cycled again into the awareness and concern of humanity. One small way of contributing to this global ideal is to introduce semantic analysis, correction, and invention into the science and art of working oracles.

Earlier we mentioned how linguistic phrases contain inherent presuppostions. We emphasized the importance of examining every statement or thought presented to an oracle, and strongly urged the consultee to be sure of its appropriateness.

For an error in the statement or thought construct presented to an oracle can lead to an answer that may be damagingly misleading or empty of meaning.

Our everyday language has what semanticist Dr. Harry L. Weinberg calls an "elementalistic structure." It is comprised of a "polar structure" and a "static structure," which he defines as follows: "The first means that we split verbally that which cannot be split nonverbally; the implication is that because it can be done verbally it must be so on the nonverbal level." He gives examples: "we argue about heredity versus environment and physical versus mental. Verbally, we can discuss heredity as if it existed apart from the environment and the physical body as if it existed apart from the mind. But when we make observations, nowhere do we find an organism without an environment or a mind without a body; rather, we discover all these factors inextricably interwoven and interconnected. . . . But because we can split them verbally, the implication of the language is such that we think we will find these splits in nature. So we look for them, and not finding them, warp our findings to fit our maps instead of changing the maps to fit the findings."

Our polar, two-valued language structure is burdened with terms such as good-bad, black-white, beautiful-ugly, large-small, tall-short, etc. Such terms imply a simplicity not found in reality. Once we fully understand this, it should enable us to work oracles so that they become a practical and healthy exercise within the process of living, instead of a gimmick resorted to during interludes of hopeless confoundment and abandonment of rationality.

Intuition plays an important role in interpreting oracles. What kind of awareness does a word, a phrase, a color spark in consciousness? And what about the symbols introduced by oracles? As we interpret, what metaphoric parallels do they inspire? Oracles may be more than instruments of intuition. We should ponder often on this very rich paragraph in philosopher-scientist Dr. R. G. H. Siu's *The Tao of Science:*

Yet even intuitive knowledge itself is not the ultimate stretch. Sooner or later we hesitate at the limits of rational and

intuitive knowledge. Our faltering mind must then seek repose and cure in what it cannot know. At this point the concept of sage-knowledge or no-knowledge is introduced by the Taoists. This is really not knowledge in the ordinary sense. Knowledge, as we understand it in the West, involves the selection of a certain event or quality as the object of knowledge. Sage-knowledge does not do so. It concerns an understanding of what the East calls Wu or nonbeing. The Wu transcends events and qualities; it has no shape, no time. As a result it cannot be the object of ordinary knowledge. At the higher level of cognizance, the sage forgets distinctions between things. He lives in the silence of what remains in the undifferentiable whole.

It seems to me that the above allows us to suggest the possibility that there may be a significant alliance here with the Golden Oracle.

CHAPTER 4

Chance, Cycles, and Synchronicity

The Chinese title of this work translates as *The Living Buddha Pointing The Way To Prosperity*. We have chosen to title this first English translation of the Chinese text differently. The reasoning that motivated this decision came with the recognition that many Westerners are emotionally and intellectually influenced and conditioned by the vocabularies of Judeo-Christian-Islamic theologies.

The popular translation of "Buddha," as a generic title, defines "an enlightened one," or "awakened one." It's a descriptive, not a name. The aim of this book is to acquaint you with the dynamics of this particular system, long used by the Chinese, for psychologically activating one's intuitive sensitivity to where it becomes experiencable as conscious communication.

Much of Chinese thought and practice is founded upon a few fundamental concepts that have been used for thousands of years. They have been highly effective in developing an understanding of complex as well as simple processes of physical, emotional, anatomical, intellectual, spiritual, terrestrial, and cosmic conditions. Included in these concepts are:

WEI WU WEI (爲無爲) **The Doctrine of Action through Nonaction**
YIN-YANG (陰 陽) **The Principle of Polarity**
WU XING (五 行) **The Five Elements**
BA GUA (八 卦) **The Interaction of the Eight Forces**

23

In Chinese culture, these have been among the most significant basic conceptual premises influencing human thought and shaping the culture's understanding of life. These same remarkable concepts have also been used for helping the individual to become prosperous. Prosperity—that is what this book deals with. Prosperity is every person's golden dream.

Whether we call it prosperity, profit motive, gain incentive, or golden chance, the idea of attaining a degree of some kind of economic, moral, emotional, intellectual, or spiritual affluence is a common goal of most people. Most of us want to find ways of attracting prosperity. Our language is filled with imagery indicating the inseparable alliance between gold and wealth: *the goose that laid the golden egg, the golden bird, the golden rule.* In short, we want to know how to become wealthy, which is often thought to be synonymous with having security. Here we have given a new name to this dynamic Asian heritage. This Five-Colors System, as it is sometimes called, has long been a useful and inspiring way for provoking the human mind into creative analytical performance. We concur with Shakespeare: "A rose by any other name would smell as sweet." So this literature, until now endemic to the Chinese is being presented in English for the first time under the title *The Golden Oracle.* This book presents a process of ritual and a scheme of verbal association that can be used with expectative assurance. Its system will put us on the right path to our goal and serve to warn us when we are not on the right path. Centuries ago, Chinese thought contended that which modern quantum physics is just discovering. We are not outside observers, but inseparable participators in a cosmic operation of energy and intelligence that is intricately interconnected. The viewpoint presented in this work emphasizes the deeper actuality that experience is an internal-external summation of events that occurs subjectively in consciousness. It differs from the old, continuing Western view that interprets consciousness as an external event reacted to by an internal response. Indeed, there is a great difference between noting the beauty of a tree or flower "over there" and a cloud formation "up there," and the deeply broader perception that *I am consciously able to enjoy the beauty of my flowerness, my treeness, my cloudness* or

24

whatever it may be. To recognize internally the "beingness" of what is perceived as external is to experience at infrequent, surprising moments the divine euphoria of cosmic consciousness.

The system offered in this book constitutes a method for psychologically and metaphysically activating one's intuition so that it registers and manifests in consciousness. Thus, one is able to pre-sense the conditions that will influence the nature of matters dealing with one's career, proposed undertakings, emotions, and other personal concerns. Through the use of your intuition, you can exercise intelligent perceptiveness in designing and planning activity that will embrace the possibility of success and good fortune.

As you apply the system delineated in this book, we believe you will come to marvel at how it stimulates mental processes of creative analysis. The products of these analyses can be translated into correct positive action befitting a specific situation. We have added some pages of necessary explanation so that you may understand its *modus operandi*.

The system involves factors of *chance, cycles,* and *synchronicity.* This being so, let's begin by clarifying and deepening our understanding of each factor of this trinity.

We all have something of an idea of what is meant by *chance, cycles,* and *synchronicity.* Through a simplified study of these concepts such as we are about to introduce, we will be able to arrive at one of many explanations possible as to how this unique parapsychological contrivance of Chinese invention works.

Let us begin with the concept of chance. In the space that follows, define *chance* as you understand its meaning. Do this before reading on.

Now read the following collection of statements concerning the concept of chance.

Ecclesiastes 9:11: I returned and saw under the sun, that the race is not to the swift, nor the battle to the strong, neither yet bread to the wise, nor yet riches to men of understanding, nor yet favor to men of skill; but time and chance happeneth to them all.

JOHN MILTON, *Comus* 587: That power which erring men call chance.

VOLTAIRE: Chance is a word void of sense; nothing can exist without a cause.

GEORGE SAND, *Handsome Lawrence II*: Discouragement seizes us only when we can no longer count on chance.

WILLIAM COWPER, *Conversation*: A fool must now and then be right by chance.

KHIGH DHIEGH, *The Eleventh Wing*: Because our dictionaries list among several synonyms for chance the word "accident," it is always offered as an explanation of what "chance" is .... think out the implications of this declaration: "Accident may happen by chance, but chance never happens by accident."[6]

Someone once defined chance as "an actuality for which the cause has not yet been discovered."

CARL GUSTAV JUNG, *Collected Works*, Vols. 2 and 7: We must admit that there is something to be said for the immense importance of chance. An incalculable amount of human

---

[6]Khigh Dhiegh, Ph.D.: *The Eleventh Wing*, Nash: California, 1973.

effort is directed to combatting and restricting the nuisance or danger that chance represents. Theoretical considerations of cause and effect often look pale and dusty in comparison with the practical results of chance.

The irrationality of events is shown in what we call chance, which we are obviously compelled to deny, because we cannot, in principle, think of any process that is not causal and necessary, whence it follows that it cannot happen by chance. In practice, however, chance reigns everywhere, and so obtrusively that we might as well put our causal philosophy in our pocket.[7]

To conclude this section, here is some statistical information about the term *chance*. It occurs only six times in the Bible, and once as *chanceth*, making seven mentions in all. Yet, as Jung points out, chance is a vital part of our daily experience. On the other hand, *cause* appears in the texts of the Bible 272 times, 32 times as *causeth*, 7 times in the plural form *causes*, 4 times as *causing*, and twice as *causest*. To complete the statistic, the negative *causeless*, appears twice. This makes some 317 mentions in the Bible, in one form or another, of the term *cause*, as against only 7 mentions of *chance*. Is it any wonder that our Western culture has been so predominantly preoccupied with the concept of causality while spending most of its time trying to avoid the consequences of chance?

In the space below restate your idea of the concept of chance, incorporating any thoughts which you may have found in the foregoing quotations which may have refined, deepened, or broadened your original statement about chance.

[7]Carl G. Jung, Ph.D.: *Collected Works, Vols. II, VIII,* Bollingen Series XX, Princeton University Press: New Jersey, 1958. Excerpt reprinted by permission of Princeton University Press.

In this next space, write down your definition of *cycles.*
Try to include your idea of what the function of cycles is in
the scheme of existence.

Now let us see if your original statement will in any way
be affected by the following collection of quotations dealing
with the subject of cycles:

MIRCEA ELIADE, *Eranos Yearbooks*: The myth of cyclical
Time—of the cosmic cycles that repeat themselves ad infin-
itum—is not an innovation of Indian speculation. . . . The
traditional societies conceive of man's temporal existence
not only as an infinite repetition of certain archetypes and
exemplary gestures but also as an eternal renewal. In symbols and ritual the world is re-created periodically.

28

What is the meaning of these myths and rites? Their central meaning is that the world is born, grows weary, perishes, and is born anew in a precipitate rhythm. . . . For the most evident periodicity is that of the moon, and it was terms relating to the moon which first served to express the measurement of time. The lunar rhythms always mark a "creation" (the new moon) followed by a "growth" (the full moon), and a diminution and "death" (the three moonless nights). It is most probably the image of this eternal birth and death of the moon that helped to crystallize early man's intuitions concerning the periodicity of life and death, and subsequently gave rise to the myths of the periodic creation and destruction of the world.[8]

China's oldest literary work that has survived up to the present day is *I Ching*. It is commonly translated as "The Book of Changes." The author-philosopher Ch'eng Hao, in the eleventh century, wrote that the *I Ching* deals with nothing but the principle of reversion, of coming and going, and of rise and fall.

CHU HSI (1130–1200): In the way of Yin and Yang, each advance is followed by a withdrawal and each increase is followed by a decrease. Reversion, coming and going, and rise and fall, can be seen in this process.

WANG YANG-MING, *Instructions for Practical Living*: Spring and summer are ceaseless in their course. So are autumn and winter. In this respect they may both be regarded as cases of Yang activity. The substance of spring and summer is eternal. So is that of autumn and winter. In this respect they may both be regarded as cases of Yin and tranquillity. The same may be said of a cycle, an epoch, a revolution, a generation, a year, a month, a day, or a period down to a minute, a second, or an infinitesimal duration. Activity and

---

[8]Joseph Campbell, ed.: *Spirit and Nature: Papers from the Eranos Yearbooks, vol. I,* Bollingen Series XXX, Princeton University Press: New Jersey, 1954. Excerpt reprinted by permission of Princeton University Press.

tranquillity have no beginning, and Yin and Yang have no starting point.[9]

According to Shao Yung (1101–1177), a generation is a period of 30 years, a revolution is a period of 12 generations, an epoch is a period of 30 revolutions, and a cycle is a period of 30 epochs.

From a scientific point of view, one will recognize that the ancient Taoists postulated what closely approximates a modern theory of evolution in their descriptions of cataclysmic cycles. A popular passage appears in the eighteenth chapter of *Chuang Tzu*. Ancient Greek writings promote the same concept.

XENOPHANES as quoted by HIPPOLYTUS: Xenophanes says that the sea is salt because a great variety of mixed materials flow into it. He further says that the land and sea were once mixed up, and even thinks that the land is dissolved in course of time by moisture. For this he says he has the following proofs. Shells [of sea animals] are found far inland and on mountains, and he tells us that in the stone quarries at Syracuse imprints [remains] of fish and a certain kind of seaweed have been found, while at Paros in the depths of the rock there are impressions of sardines, and at Malta similar moulds of all kinds of marine creatures. He says that it follows from this that at one time all these lands were under water. After all things had been turned into mud, the impressions were dried out and consolidated. And men must all perish when the earth has been carried down into the sea and [again] become mud; and from that point generation will begin anew, and these changes take place in all the world.

Once we pause and try to identify and list them, we will find an almost inexhaustible number of kinds of cycles. There is the compartmentalization of the year into recurring units of 12 months, the repetitive 4 seasons, the 7 days of the week (the Chinese once used a 10-day week), night and day, phases

[9]Wang Yang-Ming: *Instructions for Practical Living,* Columbia University Press: New York, 1963.

of the moon, the tides of lakes, rivers, seas, and oceans. To these and the kinds of cycles we experience personally. These include our heartbeat, sleeping and waking, hunger and satiety, respiration, the female menstrual cycle, the circulation of blood, and so on. This list can be added to by naming cycles of evolutionary processes, cataclysimic cycles, and cycles of the rise and fall of nations.

In the space that follows rewrite your statement about cycles, modifying or enlarging it according to how the above quotations have influenced your thinking.

Before reading on, write down your idea of what is meant by the term *synchronicity*.

By now you will have discovered that this method of progressive participation has activated your own creative and productive instincts.

By relating intuitive methodologies to the new thinking of scholarly and scientific minds, we hope to encourage you to develop your individual cosmic-conscious instincts.[1] Through the writings now shared with the public, we are discovering that there is a remarkable affinity between so-called "Asian mystic visions of reality" and the actual universe being revealed through the research activities of modern physics.

As Dr. Bolen notes: "The picture of an interconnected cosmic web in which the human observer is always a participator emerges from quantum physics. At the atomic particle level, the world view becomes very Eastern and mystical; time and space become a continuum, matter and energy interchange, observer and observed interact."[10] This revelation helps to clarify the concerns of synchronicity. For synchronicity requires a human participant (yourself), for all consciously perceived experience (the text comprising this system), which is given meaning by your responsive consciousness, which is initially and ultimately subjective.

Keep this in mind as you read the following collection of quotations relating to synchronicity. Prepare yourself to make another statement about synchronicity that will reflect the influence, if any, of the following quotations.

The term *synchronicity* was coined by Carl Gustav Jung. He invented it to make understandable to Western readers certain fundamental psycho-phenomenal concepts held in areas of Chinese philosophy which are demonstrable in the workings of the ancient classic *I Ching* ("The Book of Changes"). Jung noted that his concept of synchronicity would be almost wholly unintelligent to Chinese thought systems. However, those of his readers who could understand what it was pointing to,

[10]Jean Shinoda Bolen, M.D.: *The Tao of Psychology,* Harper & Row: New York, 1979.

would, in consequence, have a better understanding of Chinese thought and metaphysical processes. The following quotations are about synchronicity:

CARL JUNG, *Eranos Yearbook*: I mean by synchronicity . . . the not uncommonly observed "coincidence" of subjective and objective happenings, which just cannot be explained causally, at least in the present state of our knowledge. On this premise astrology is based and the methods of *I Ching*.

Once we can rid ourselves of the highly unscientific pretense that it is merely a question of chance coincidence, we shall see that synchronistic phenomena are not unusual occurrences at all, but are relatively common, not to say banal. This fact is in entire agreement with Rhine's "probability-exceeding" results. The psyche is not a chaos made up of random whims and accidents, but is an objective reality to which the investigator can gain access by the methods of natural science. There are indications that psychic processes stand in some sort of energy relation to the physiological substrate. These processes, so far as they are objective events, can hardly be interpreted as anything but energy processes, or to put it another way: in spite of the non-measurability of psychic processes, the perceptible changes effected by the psyche cannot possibly be understood except as a phenomenon of energy.

The causality principle asserts that the connection between cause and effect is a necessary one. The synchronicity principle asserts that the terms of a meaningful coincidence are connected by simultaneity and meaning. So if we assume that the ESP experiments and numerous other observations are established facts, we must conclude that besides the connection between cause and effect there is another factor in nature which expresses itself in the arrangement of events and appears to us as meaning. Although meaning is an anthropomorphic interpretation it nevertheless forms the indispensable criterion of synchronicity. What that factor which appears to us as "meaning" may be in itself we have no possibility of knowing. As an hypothesis, however, it is not quite so impossible as may appear at first sight. We must remember that the rationalistic attitude of the West is not the only possible one and is not all-embracing, but is in many ways a prejudice and a bias that ought perhaps to be corrected.

It is like this: you are standing on the seashore and the waves wash up an old hat, an old box, a shoe, a dead fish, and there they lie on the shore. You say: "Chance, nonsense!" The Chinese mind asks: "What does it mean that these things are together?" The Chinese mind experiments with that being together and coming together at the right moment, and it has an experimental method which is not known in the West, but which plays a large role in the philosophy of the East. It is a method of forecasting possibilities, and it is still used by the Japanese Government about political situations; it was used, for instance, in the Great War. This method was formulated in 1143 B.C.

Just as causality describes the sequence of events, so synchronicity to the Chinese mind deals with the coincidence of events.[11]

JOLANDE JACOBI, *Complex/Archetype/Symbol in the Psychology of Jung*: The studies and investigations that Jung has long devoted to these phenomena have led him in the last few years to assume the existence of a novel principle of nature, which manifests itself under definite psychic conditions. "Space, time, and causality, the triad of classical physics," he writes, "would then be supplemented by the synchronicity factor and become a tetrad." In contradistinction to "synchronism" (simultaneity) he called this principle "synchronicity." By this he wished to designate "a coincidence in time of two or more causally unrelated events which have a similar meaning"; this applies also to all "a priori factors" or "acts of creation in time." However incomprehensible it may appear, we are finally compelled to assume

[11]Joseph Campbell, ed.: *Spirit and Nature: Papers from the Eranos Yearbooks, vol. I,* Bollingen Series XXX, Princeton University Press: New Jersey, 1954. Excerpt reprinted by permission of Princeton University Press.

that there is in the unconscious something like an a priori knowledge or an 'immediacy' of events which lacks any causal basis, but which manifests itself wherever the constellation is suitable. In this connection Jung goes back to the old, never satisfactorily solved problem of psychophysical parallelism, examining it from a new point of view and attempting to give it new meaning.

Synchronicity, he writes, "possesses properties that may help to clear up the body-soul problem. Above all it is the fact of causeless order, or rather, of meaningful orderedness, that may throw light on the psychophysical parallelism."

With the benefit of these descriptive passages on synchronicity, compose, in the space below, a fresh statement of what you think is meant by *synchronicity*.

Now, let us put this together and show how it is a part of this unique Chinese system which includes the act of mixing, casting, and blindly arranging five discs on five different colored squares, three times. Using the numerically identified passage

[12]Jolande Jacobi: *Complex/Archetype/Symbol in the Psychology of C.G. Jung,* trans. Ralph Manheim, Bollingen Series LVII, Princeton University Press: New Jersey, 1959. Excerpt reprinted by permission of Princeton University Press.

of a text that interprets the symbology assigned to that cast, one can reason out a meaningful insight into a personally selected concern. The conviction underlying this practice is that it will be successful in awakening a kind of heightened insight that results in a clarification of understanding, acceptance, and certitude being experienced, so that coping with the matter of concern is possible.

The factor of *chance* is a part of this system. The three castings of the five coins or discs constitute a chance method (this differs from probability), or arriving at a particular pattern of color sequence that determines which of the 125 identified texts is applicable to the consultation.

An important concept underlying Chinese philosophy is that all life, all existence, all knowledge, and all ignorance is in a constant state of change. Change has three primary forms. It manifests as sequential, cyclical, and as non-change. You will recognize one of each of these forms in the following chapter. These examples will help you make other identifications.

CHAPTER 5

The Development of Oracles

It is reported that Theodore Roosevelt, the 26th president of the United States, had a plaque on his desk which read: "Example demonstrates the possibility of success." That is the purpose of this chapter. Here we shall forego the disuse of the Aristotelian *is* of identity, and use all the other *"is's"* too. You will find that this chapter reads with easier comprehension. However, we shall continue to provoke and, if necessary, cajole you into feeling, thinking, and seeing afresh. The purpose of this chapter is to enable you to accomplish and experience these conditions by presenting you with a brief series of examples of the Golden Oracle. Following each example, we will give suggestions and guidance to help you work the oracle in a comparatively similar, but personal, context. A brief synoptic reflection on the role of oracles throughout history is included as background material. In this way, you will not just be reading or watching the process. Instead, individually and subjectively, you will be using this oracle in a variety of ways and experiencing it personally.

This chapter will be concerned with a number of different usages possible with the Golden Oracle. By *usage* we mean customary procedures and standard methods of use as established by repetitive societal practice. We, the authors, can attest that one experiences a euphoric stimulation in consciousness when using the Golden Oracle for heightening one's intuitive perceptiveness.

Oracles date back to the earliest known literate societies. It is reasonable to presume that the practice of oracle consultation predates the ability of humans to express vocal symbols through the use of graphic representation. During the latter part of the second millennium B.C., people living under the Shang dynasty made little or no speculation on where they went after death. They did, however, exhibit a pronounced concern about the attitude of family spirits. This is evidenced by the great number of oracle bone inscriptions inquiring to know whether or not particular illnesses or misfortunes were due to the dissatisfaction of particular ancestral spirits.

Joseph Needham, in his monumental work *Science and Civilization in China*, notes that before there was a written *I Ching*, there was the tortoise shell oracle. Archaeological findings indicate that during the period of the most remote antiquity of Chinese history, oracles were consulted for guidance, confirmation, and inspiration. Many different kinds of things have furnished the means for devising oracles. In China there have been tortoise shells, scapula bones, Fung-Shui (geomancy), *I Ching*, Golden Oracle, and so forth.

In other traditions, such as the Hebrew, we find a wide range of trees serving as oracle sources. In the fifth chapter of the second book of Samuel, it is written: "And when David inquired of the Lord, he said, Thou shalt not go up; but fetch a compass behind them, and come upon them over against the mulberry trees. And let it be, when thou hearest the sound of a going in the tops of the mulberry trees, that then thou shalt bestir thyself; for then shall the Lord go out before thee, to smite the host of the Philistines." Here "the sound of a going in the tops of the mulberry trees" constituted the oracular sign.

It may be worth mentioning that "tree oracles" were not solely a province of the ancient Jews. At the famous oracle at Dodona on Mount Tomarus, Epirus, in ancient Greece, the rustling of the oak leaves was used and interpreted to give the meaning of the oracle.

Oracles can be discovered as spontaneous individual phenomena, or they can be tutored, being traditional institutionalized systems for provoking insight and enlightenment. It is interesting that in the Old Testament, the term oracle appears

17 times, while in the New Testament, it appears only 4 times. *Oracle*, as a word, never appears in the body of the Gospels even though there are many and varied alludings to things which are "signs" and "omens."

In the Judeo-Christian traditions, as in all others, oracles are recognized as being responses and revelations of gods, and have been sought in many different ways. Jehovah responded through the mysterious media of Urim and Thummim. These devices, common in the biblical era, are recorded as having been placed on the breastplates of the high priests as mediums for the revelation of the will of God to his people.

Throughout history oracles have been alternately praised and damned. At times, they have been simultaneously accepted and rejected, revered and denounced. Herodotus, the Greek historian (484?–425 B.C.), was known to have had a fascination for all manner of recognized and ambiguous oracles. Historians tell us that Asclepius, the son of Apollo, learned by oracles what drugs to employ for different diseases and in what amounts to mix the drugs so they will be most effective. He also learned what the antidotes for poisons were and even how to use poisons as remedies. Then there was the emperor Julian (A.D. 331–363), who believed in almost every form of divination. In fact, he ascribed to the oracles of Apollo the victory of Greek civilization over the greater part of the then-known world.

Astrampsychos, who is supposed to have been one of the Persian Magi, was first mentioned by Diogenes Laertius in the early third century. He is credited with having authored a secret book of oracles addressed to Ptolemy. Later, in the medieval period, Caspar Pencer (1525–1602), who authored several books on medicine, astronomy, mathematics, natural history, and so forth, and first published at Wittenberg in 1553, quoted numerous passages from the ancient oracles in his attacks upon what he felt to be spurious revelation. He contended that the oldest oracles, such as those of Jupiter, Ammon in Egypt, and of Dodona, were all perversions affected by the devil. He claimed these oracles were rooted in the domestic school which Noah established after the flood, for his children and grandchildren. They later set up similar schools as they roamed over the expanse of the globe. He felt that these schools were gradually perverted into the seats of oracles which owed their efficacy to the darkest diabolic forces.

We suspect that evidence supporting the claim that oracle seats were rooted in the schools established by Noah is quite limited. However, a very popular contemporary oracle device dates back to more than twenty-five hundred years ago. The modern model enjoys lucrative sales in amusement specialties shops and the games section in department stores. It is called a Ouija Board. The name can be translated into English as a "yes yes board," being a pairing of the French *oui* and the German *ja*. I remember reading, long years ago, the writings of a French historian who connected the Ouija Board with the Greek philosopher, Pythagoras (died about 497 B.C.). He told of a sect to which Pythagoras belonged, which held seances. At these gatherings they used a mysterious table that moved on wheels toward prearranged signs. Pythagoras and his pupil, Philolaus, would interpret the movings to the assembled audience, presenting them as being revelations communicated from an unseen world. This brief account surely suggests not only the antiquity of oracles, but also that some forms of them have continued to be used right up to the present day. So let us return to our Golden Oracle and give some examples of how it may be worked, in our time, for our purposes.

Our demonstration shall be limited to three kinds of usage even though there are many more. The following three examples should be sufficient to fire our imagination and inspire us to dare.

Example 1. Selecting a good-luck name for a person, business, animate or inanimate thing.

Example 2. Selecting a good-luck hour, day, date, or time for traveling, buying, selling, vacationing, partying, speaking, or taking an examination.

Example 3. Using the oracle for general consultation as an aid in heightening one's intuitive insights concerning the prospects for any planned activity one anticipates being involved with.

Some of the traditional rituals and other requirements customary for working this Golden Oracle are not only quite complicated, but also uniquely indigenous to Chinese culture. Among the Chinese consultees, individual convictions vary greatly. Some believe that one's astrological data must be included with every consultation. For others who disagree, there will be many different kinds of specific information and ritually required observances deemed essential for a successful working of the oracle. These differences are often confounding even to the Chinese. Therefore we shall forego any further mention of them. Instead, let us turn our attention to the simplest and most ritualistically relaxed method of addressing the oracle. It is the method used by a great majority of Chinese. In adapting the method about to be described, we shall be conforming in practice and procedure with what is most broadly prescribed by tradition.

SELECTING A GOOD-LUCK NAME

We shall hypothesize that we are opening a Chinese restaurant and want to memorialize a distinguished historical personage by identifying the restaurant with his name. Of course, we want to feel that the name selected will attract good fortune, so that our business venture will be financially successful. The first name chosen has been arbitrarily taken from a volume of writings which happen to be on the desk before me, as I am writing this. It is the name of Han Fei, the legalist of the second century B.C.

Han Fei was one of the princes of the Han State, who was reputedly fond of studies in penology, epistemology, law, and statecraft. He proudly traced his principles back to the Yellow Emperor and the sage Lao Tzu. He was known to be a stutterer. He was incapable of delivering fluent speeches, but he was very proficient in law and in writing books. But we must return to selecting a name for our restaurant by turning to the Golden Oracle.

We write out the name Han Fei, which in Chinese char-

41

acters appears thus: 韓非 . It takes 26 strokes to structure the name. Turning to page 80 in the text, we find number 26 at the top of a list of 25 oracle responses which have in common that they all begin at the top with the color yellow. The synoptic comment reads: "Power of earth is great. Regard ancestors."

What has happened is astounding. When I began composing this example, I had no idea of a name. As it has already been stated, on the desk before me was a volume of Han Fei's writings. The name was selected with no knowledge of how many strokes it contained, nor where in the oracle it would numerically match. Share with me the surprise that it is both positive and promising according to the brief comment in the identification charts. But how significantly unique that part of that brief phrasing should read "Regard ancestors!"

Looking up the 26th oracle response we find "Yellow, Yellow, Yellow. Up and Up."

EXPLANATION: With three Yellows in a row, the power of earth is great indeed. Great joy and good fortune. All things are nourished and sustained. The consultee has received well from the ancestor and will leave sustained wealth for the descendants. Good fortune without end.

JUDGMENT: Long lasting wealth and prosperity. Heavens respond to cultivated virtue. Portends good fortune, longevity, and many descendants.

COMMENTARY: The text assigned this image is indeed euphoric. A superficial reading of it, however, may miss the deeper implications, which are indeed desirable. The phrase "had received well from the ancestor" refers not alone to financial and/or property gains, but to the examples, the teachings, the heritage in a much broader sense. Ancestor is not necessarily a reference to a blood relative, but to that which preceded. After all, there is a popular belief among many people that we all are descended from a common ancestor.

This response or synchronistic paralleling is so excitingly encouraging that one may be tempted to run out at once and open the Han Fei Restaurant of Princely Cuisine. In this instance, the relevancies seem to be blatantly applicable. There is hardly a need to draw metaphoric comparisons. "All things are nourished and sustained" is immediately identified with restaurants and food.

This translation of the Golden Oracle is designed for the use of Westerners. Not too many of those using this text are going to be accomplished in reading and writing Chinese. But this Golden Oracle can be worked using other systems of graphic expression representing names and thoughts. For example, let us hypothesize that I am interested in naming a newborn son. I am uncertain about naming him as a Junior, and am considering the names Alx Dhiegh, Khigh Alx Dhiegh Junior and Khigh Dhiegh. I will first print out all of the names in Roman block letters. For the first selection mentioned above I will have 21 strokes, 42 strokes for the second selection, and 25 strokes for the third alternate.

The first textual response is number 21, Hsia-Hsia, Low and Low. The next response, number 42, is Shang-Chung, Upper Middle. The third name comes to 25, Chung Ping, Middle. A quick reference to the Casting Identification Charts informs us that number 21 advises "seek to avoid." Number 42 responds with "wealth properly attained." And number 25 offers the prediction of "a good change in fortune." From this, I would feel advised not to name my son Alx Dhiegh, but to choose between the second and third alternatives.

SELECTING A GOOD-LUCK DAY OR TIME

Many Chinese consult the red almanac published annually in Hong Kong to learn if a time (hour, day, and so on) is propitious for a particular activity. Another way is to cast the discs or coins to structure a color pattern that will indicate the quality of efficacy of the time for a specific purpose. Yet another method is to print out the matter of concern in block letters and count the strokes made in completing the statement. For

43

example, Ed Grinns, the Happy Mortician, is curious about his vacation. He prints out his concern thusly: "Vacation from August sixteenth to thirtieth."

It took 82 strokes to print out the phrase in Roman letters. When we turn to oracle response number 82, we discover it is Chung Ping, Middle. You may turn to the full text on page (136). Reporting on it quickly, it warns to avoid over-ambitiousness and cautions one to utilize prosperity. I shall leave it to the reader to study the Explanation and Judgment texts and to structure a personal interpretation, while I will interpret only what is written in the Commentary. And this interpretation applies to only this hypothetical instance.

That it is a middle category casting suggests that the time is quite appropriate for vacationing. However, going on a vacation is not usually seen as an opportunity to deliberately further one's career. But by displaying a knack for efficient planning, he may catch the interest of an influential person at the same site in a way that could lead to a rewarding relationship at a later time. He should, therefore, be alert in social contacts and avoid voicing negative feelings or unhappiness with his current business affiliation. He should not become flamboyant or overly extravagant. To do so will reflect poorly and foster doubt in others of his real abilities and talents.

MAKING A GENERAL CONSULTATION

The previous examples of usage of the Golden Oracle are of a kind that solicits meaning by establishing a mechanical correspondence. That is, the numbered oracle response applicable to the given situation is mechanically determined by the number of strokes necessary to mark out the graphic representation of the situation with which the consultee is concerned. The mechanical paralleling of the total number of strokes with the oracle response number generates a processing in mind that enables the consultee to discover meaningful instruction and information concealed in the discursive symbolic forms of that particular oracular correspondence.

A general consultation differs from the examples given above. Here the worker of the oracle is not as much concerned with discovering meaningful instruction and information concealed in the mechanical correspondence between the graphically represented situation and the oracle response, as in that the oracle response shall activate in them an intuitive perception and talent for metaphoric analysis. The desire is intensely strong that they shall become enriched with a creative insight on the substance, its time, and the dynamics of all the other aspects of the situation in which they are involved.

To illustrate, let us postulate a situation in which I want to produce a play at the local community theatre. There is evidence of general interest and enthusiasm for the project among the public. But experience has taught that this can quickly dwindle into empty verbiage when you begin approaching people for definite commitments of talent, time, labor, and money. So before organizing the project, I want to have the advantage of exploring the possible textures of the actualities that will evolve with the materialization of the idea to produce a play at the local community theatre. For this purpose, one will do well by complying with the general instructions in the next chapter.

CHAPTER 6

How to Work the Golden Oracle

Particulars for working the Golden Oracle in accord with traditional observances and practices follows:

THE REQUIRED MATERIALS

Five coins or discs of equal size are needed. One of these should be distinguishable from the others by having a red marking. As a substitute, if one is using five coins, let four of them be dull, the stand-out coin being shiny.

Also needed are three sticks of incense (preferably the long Chinese sandlewood joss type), a censer filled with a combination of rice and sand, matches, two candlestick holders, and two red candles.

APPROPRIATE TIME

Customarily, any time of day or night is alright, excepting for the "vacant" hours, which can be identified by consulting a Chinese Energy Calendar, such as appears in the *I Ching: Taoist Book of Days*. Tradition holds that the early morning hours are the most efficacious.

THE PROCEDURE

Every sincere intention to work the Golden Oracle should be hallowed by first cleansing the body. After the body has been reverently bathed, prepare to activate this method of heightening your intuitive awareness by purifying the mind.

Mind is that condition of consciousness wherein our thinking manifests. That which we think is recognized as thought. Thought may be regarded as being motivated in great part by our individual accumulation of pre-birth and post-birth experiences, beliefs, and desires, as influenced by the long-enduring humanity that operates through us. Thought is not alienated from the cosmic purposiveness that inheres in all creation. All human thought originates in both our mortal humanness and our immortal soul.

Purifying the mind does not mean directing our consciousness beyond the everydayness of this world. Purification of the mind has very little to do with alienating ourselves from this existence. Purifying the mind is not forcing oneself into a stupor of vacuity. The spiritual world is this one. The divine life is our everyday experience.

Purifying the mind has to do with the explication of consciousness in harmonic resonance with nature. Purifying the mind is reaching beyond the duality and trying to sense and touch the *unity*, the *ultimate form of no form*. Purifying the mind is to envelop the meaning of meaning; it is to see the shape of shape.

When you feel blissfully composed and floatingly comfortable, light the two red candles. These symbolize the negative and positive energy forces, the yin and yang mystery, the is and is-not of all existing things and beings. Hold yourself in composure and light the three sticks of incense, placing them in the rice-and-sand-filled censer.

1. Next place the five coins or discs between the palms of both hands in the gesture of prayer, preparatory to meditating. First, speak aloud your name, announcing your date and place of birth, followed by your present address. Pray for a congenial communication and response; that is, explain the purpose of your asking for instruction and counsel concerning the matter that is uppermost in your mind. Focus upon the issue and accept with expectation that you shall experience a revelatory and penetrating insight and deep understanding of that which you are concentrating upon.

Now position your palms so that they are cupped one within the other, holding the five coins loosely between them. Shake the coins well, then grasp them in one hand or the other. With-

2. out looking at them, place them one at a time in the large colored squares on page.* starting with the red square at the top and moving downward to the black square at the bottom.

3. Repeat this process three times," each time noting the color the odd coin or disc rests upon." Use R = Red, Y = Yellow, B = Blue,

4. W = White and N = Black. When you have a combination of three colors, constituting a pronouncement, check it against the index in the back pages of the book, where you will find

5. displayed the correct oracle response number. Turn to the numbered response in the oracle text to read the oracle's statement concerning your situation.

At this time you need to be fully receptive and sensitive. The input of cosmic intelligence is communicated as vibrations of knowing and recognition via the symbols and metaphors in the content of the oracle's pronouncement.

We return to the concern of wanting to produce a play in the local community theater. How will such a venture fare? After following the instructions given in this chapter, I chanced upon the color symbol of White-Black-White, number 96, Shang-Shang, Up and Up.

The synoptic statement reads: "Metal generates water abundantly. There can be quick success." The reader can turn to the oracle response number 96 and read the pronouncement's Explanation, Judgment, and Commentary. Upon reading it, you will become aware that with all the abounding help and awaiting good fortune, there is one very important requirement: the consultee "must be extraordinarily perspicacious in selecting a project to promote." If the consultee fails to meet this requirement, all the positive energy nearby can evaporate into

*colored squares on back cover .

wishful longing. Here once again, the reader will note that the consultee cannot absent himself or herself from the energy process of the cosmic design.

THE TEXT

In the original Chinese text, of *Living Buddha Pointing the Way to Prosperity*, the following characters are used to give an evaluative description to the casting made:

上 (shang):   Up, upon, superior, to mount
下 (xia):   Below, to descend, inferior
中 (zhung):   Center, to hit the center, attain
平 (ping):   Even, equal, peaceful, quiet, to adjust, harmonize, weigh in scales

The original text uses these characters in combinations of pairs, and they appear one above the other, as in this text. There are five combinations of these characters used to identify the five natures of fortune which are expressed by the various three color images. The loose translations of "Up and Up," "Upper Middle," "Lower Middle," "Middle," and "Low and Low" are herewith paired with other quite correct and appropriate English words. This is to more successfully convey to the Western reader the heightened sense of movement and change that is inherent in Chinese ideograms. This is an actuality that often eludes the Westerner who is steeped in ideas of absolutes.

Up and Up	shang shang	also means mounting, superior
Upper Middle	shang zhung	also means ascending middle
Middle	zhung ping	also means balancing
Lower Middle	zhung xia	also means middle descending
Low and Low	xia xia	also means inferior, worsening

In the Casting Identification Charts (pages 181–194), R = Red, Y = Yellow, B = Blue, W = White, and N = Black.

These 5 colors can be arranged in 125 combinations of 3. Of these triune combinations, 20 symbolize patterns of cyclicity, 5 patterns of sequential order, and 5 are repetitive patterns symbolizing non-change. The remaining 95 constitute patterns of irregular assortiveness. Thirty of the 125 patterns are designated as "Up and Up," 25 as "Upper-Middle," 22 as "Lower-Middle," 25 as "Middle," and 23 as "Low and Low." Of the 20 cyclical patterns, 9 are "Up and Up," one is "Low-Middle," and one "Upper Middle." The 5 sequential patterns include "Low and Low" for 2, "Upper-Middle" for 2, and "Lower-Middle" for one.

In this English language text, the meaning or indication of each of the color triune patterns is expressed through three statements: Explanation, Judgment, and Commentary. The Explanation and Judgment statements are quotations translated directly from the the original Chinese text. The Commentary is the editor's response to the traditional Explanation and Judgment in terms of our Western consciousness today.

Chinese characters from the original text embellish each page of the English translation of the Golden Oracle. These characters represent the five colors:

紅	黃	藍	白	黑
紅	黃	藍	白	黑
紅	黃	藍	白	黑
3 Red	3 Yellow	3 Blue	3 White	3 Black

Reading from the top downward, here is an example of the system as it appears in the text.

Red

Blue

White

represents oracle pronouncement number 14

The following characters represent numerals:

One	一	Six	六	Twenty	二十	Sixty	六十
Two	二	Seven	七	Thirty	三十	Seventy	七十
Three	三	Eight	八				
Four	四	Nine	九	Forty	四十	Eighty	八十
Five	五	Ten	十	Fifty	五十	Ninety	九十
						Hundred	百

THE TRICOLOR PATTERNS

On each of the next 125 pages is printed a translation of the original Chinese text that interprets a meaning for each color combination. The color triunes are composed of from one to three of the five symbolic colors tradition has assigned to this Chinese parapsychological system.

The five colors represent the five elements. Each color triune represents one to three of the five elements in an arrangement that, intuitively read, provokes meaning. There are five kinds of arrangements. They may be described thusly:

1.   The *triple repetitive arrangement* results when the odd piece of the tossing coins or casting discs falls upon the same color with each of the three throws.

2.   The *top double repetitive arrangement* results when the odd piece of the first two tosses of the coins or casts of the discs falls upon the same color, while the last throw falls upon a different color.

3.   The *bottom double repetitive arrangement* results when the odd piece of the last two tosses of the coins or casts of the discs falls upon the same color, while the first throw falls upon a different color.

4.   The *split double repetitive arrangement* results when the odd piece of the first and last tosses of the coins or casts of the discs falls upon a different color. This also symbolizes cyclical phenomena.

5.   The *nonrepetitive sequence* results when the odd piece of each toss of the coins or cast of the discs falls upon a different color. In this arrangement, five of the castings symbolize sequential phenomena.

And, there are two kinds of sequential arrangements. The *forward-moving sequence* occurs when the color elements tossed represent a relationship conducive to a productive generating process. The *reverse-moving sequence* occurs when the color elements tossed represent a retrogressive relationship inimical to productive generation.

Part II

The Oracle Text

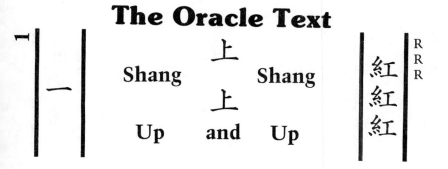

上
Shang　　　Shang
上
Up　　and　　Up

紅
紅
紅

R
R
R

EXPLANATION: When one casts Red so that it follows itself consecutively three times, it is the symbolic image of triple light. Liken it to the sun at midday. If the person utilizing this device is desiring to know a time, cosmically, the indication is for around the peak of spring (spring equinox), when the yang energy is at the maximum of its ascending energy.

JUDGMENT: One seeks prosperity and will receive prosperity. Fame and profit are both within grasp. In the cyclical order of things, progressing from spring to summer, the energy of the south is especially strong. Whatever the undertaking chosen, whether in trade or another field of activity, all affairs will have great good fortune and great profit.

COMMENTARY: The meaning here, in part, is that whatever you are especially concerned about, providing you understand it thoroughly and maintain an attitude of dedication and alertness in following up on each assertive (not aggressive) move, the time and conditions are particularly appropriate. Success is assured.

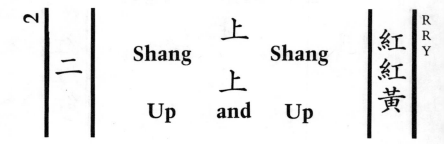

EXPLANATION: With this casting, Red comes again after Red followed by Yellow. The double Red coming first indicates a flourishing fate. Red also symbolizes fire and, preceding Yellow, gives the image of earth being born from strong fire. The position of fire is high, as in heaven, earth is low. The sages explain that in this casting, the flourishing fire yields to the submissive and complementing earth. There will be help coming from earth.

JUDGMENT: Prosperity is sure. What is sought will be obtained. But in all affairs, one must progress with diligence. Do not delay lest one miss the great opportunity.

COMMENTARY: While all the conditions that favor success are apparent, there will be a need to act with keen perceptiveness and tenacity. Keep alert to recognize those who can become future allies and who will be willing to supply whatever help may be needed when an emergency arises.

56

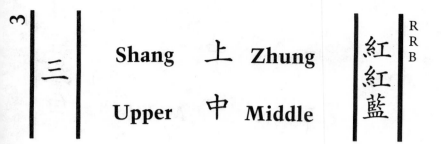

EXPLANATION: Two Reds indicates a flourishing fate. Blue is the image of wood. Combined they make up the image of a flourishing garden. Ordinarily wood generates fire. Here fire precedes wood so no generative process is taking place. Therefore a good advisement is to retreat and conserve one's means.

JUDGMENT: Since prosperity may not always be sought, there are times when it should not be sought. Prosperity often comes of itself in its proper time. Therefore recognize that in certain affairs one should employ retreat as advance. The great book says that when too full, we must invite diminishing. In the time appropriate for diminishing, one must be aware that humble reserve is often benefited.

COMMENTARY: Here one is in a situation that is viable and productive. However, it often occurs that things are in season, or height of cycle. This means that one should anticipate some kind of recession. By accepting the negative swing, we will hold secure, very much like leaning into the direction of a bicycle or motorcycle in turning. To lean against the turn is to invite an accident. So in this situation that requires diminishing, to attempt to induce flourishing may bring ruin. Wait. Help comes in the proper time.

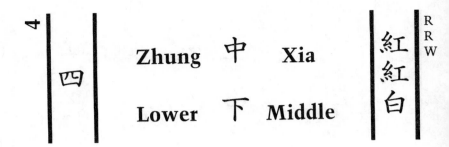

EXPLANATION: Here the two Reds are clearly fire. The one White is metal. Metal is melted by strong fire. The image symbolizes stubborn iron being checked. One should think back, review the past, and check onself. Shun situations of risk and idle speculation. Though the situation is not promising, one can still avoid loss.

JUDGMENT: The search for affluence is discouraging. Even though there may be some small gain, it will hardly match the loss. If you are about to invest, exercise great caution. Guard against the entrapment of petty people who may give cause for regret.

COMMENTARY: There is constructive and destructive fire. A bonfire always needs to be observed alertly, so that a gust of wind does not use it to start a holocaust. One should not try to toast marshmallows at a bonfire. Likewise, in life there are situations in which there are inherent dangers. An average person should not do handsprings while boating in a canoe. Even so, in speculative situations one should not act thoughtlessly.

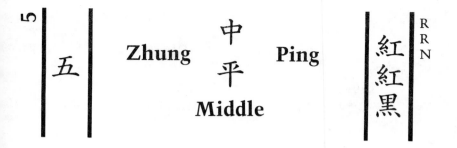

Zhung 中平 Ping

Middle

EXPLANATION: Here you have cast two Reds over one Black. In many instances, the black of water would destroy the red fire. Here, weak water is preceded by very strong fire, hence the relationship has possibilities of becoming mutually supportive. In the phenomenological process, advancing the fire will warm the water; however, in retreat the water will overcome the fire.

JUDGMENT: In the present pursuit of affluence under the given circumstances, it is essential to act decisively and speedily. Do not hesitate, meander, shrink back, or fall behind. To do so will make loss almost inevitable.

COMMENTARY: Some situations are particularly transitory. In order to cope with them constructively one needs a background of experience and familiarization that equips the person with the means of making quick decisions. What is needed is similar to the energy and know-how of speculating successfully in the stock market. One cannot take quick decisive action if one permits others to sidetrack you into considering alternatives to your knowledgeable and intuitively determined course of action.

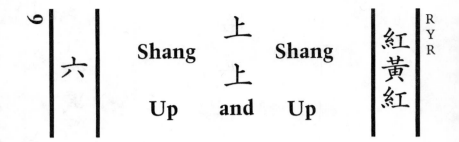

EXPLANATION: This casting yields a Yellow between two Reds: earth between fires. The general sequence is, in effect, coming or going. Here earth is efficacious, man eminent, and heaven glorious. The time has come, and fate is with the consultee. Places and conditions are appropriate. Great deeds may be accomplished.

JUDGMENT: Destiny and prosperity circulate without end, making for great affluence. Fame and fortune are both complete. Affluence and posterity will both flourish. At this time everything is developing positively. There are many to be congratulated.

COMMENTARY: The situation is basically mundane. It is presently protected front and back, and there are many forces, both people and circumstances, efficaciously interacting to promote and secure the matter at hand. It is important to publicly acknowledge the help received from eminent persons. Attention to these matters engenders success.

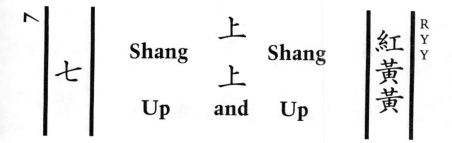

EXPLANATION: The casting of one Red followed by two Yellows is interpreted as earth being generated by fire. The image is flowers blossoming on the southern slopes. The double earth (two Yellows), is a hill; fire on top is the sun in the south. Southern slopes receive the energy of spring earliest. It is time for the return of spring. If one will ride with the time, good fortune is in one's grasp.

JUDGMENT: Seek affluence in the south. A turn of fortune comes after the winter solstice, specially favorable during the period between winter and spring. There is a great prospect of winning top honors, but one must hold on to virtue and sincerity in good fortune so that the roots can be planted deep and the blessing of wealth made lasting.

COMMENTARY: The fulfillment of one's desire is favorable. The natural conditions for progressive development are present. However, by opening an umbrella prematurely for shading oneself from the approaching summer heat, one could disrupt the present situation wherein things are all appropriately supportive of each other for great growth and desirable increase. With correct arsenalia one can be assertive (not aggressive), and enlarge friendships and opportunities.

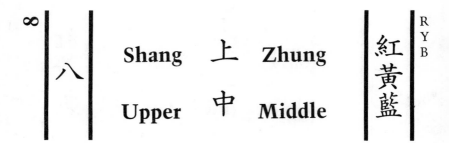

EXPLANATION: This casting has Yellow following Red, which is earth born of fire, and Blue following Yellow transforms the destructive power of wood over earth, so that it becomes supportive. This should be interpreted as indicating a flourishing fortune without need of assistance from others.

JUDGMENT: Affluence is rising to the top. One needs only to wait. No need to seek help from others. There is also the sign for receiving a son. Congratulations.

COMMENTARY: The situation has peculiarities of character. It seems that many things are growing all about, and there is the fear that one's particular interest will be thwarted. However, the surrounding growth will prove to be a protective shadow that shields your project or concern from the dehydrating effects of premature sunshine. For this reason, one should wait until success floats up to the top to crown one's efforts.

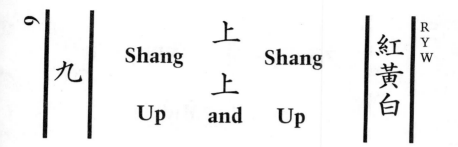

九　| |　Shang 上 Shang　紅黃白 R Y W
9
Up 上 and Up

EXPLANATION: The cast arranges Yellow following Red, which is earth born of fire. White coming after Yellow is metal born of earth. Such is the image of son and mother. It indicates continuous generation and regeneration, rising step by step.

JUDGMENT: The search for affluence is sure to be fulfilled. There will be a continuous flow and rapid progress. Very soon there may be an accumulation of wealth. One's life will be smooth, and one's affairs will terminate in accord with one's wishes.

COMMENTARY: The situation is perceived as being structured correctly for proper natural development. The yang, male, fire principle excites the yin, female, earth principle and thereby is procreated the child, renewal principle. As long as this orderly sequence prevails, there will be generation and regeneration of cherished desires. This is great good fortune.

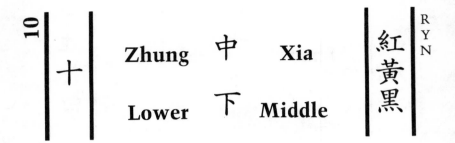

Zhung 中 **Xia**

Lower 下 **Middle**

EXPLANATION: The casting places Yellow after Red, which is earth born of fire. The Black following Yellow is water destroying earth. The image is rich fields turning into flooded marshes. The consultee should turn back to introspect and cultivate personal virtues. Do not mistake present illusions as enduring facts.

JUDGMENT: Wealth is flourishing; it comes quickly and is quickly lost. One illusory flash and all is empty. But if one can maintain calm, perhaps something may be conserved. If so, then after a brief flourishing, one may still continue.

COMMENTARY: The advantages of the situation are momentarily seen as desirable. But one should be aware that the productivity and satisfaction of the moment is after all transitory, and will not last for long. However, if one observes carefully, there are advantageous aspects of the present situation that can be conserved. By securing these positive aspects, one can continue to progress later on.

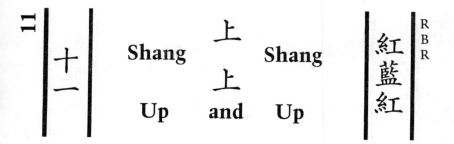

EXPLANATION: This casting situates a Blue between two Reds. The sun shines upon vegetation, and more light is generated. The image is also a blue stream flowing between banks of pink peach blossoms. The consultee may be guided into a paradise on earth.

JUDGMENT: Affluence is destined. What is sought will be received. Smooth sailing into an assured future. Help will be forthcoming. If one is investing there will be much profit.

COMMENTARY: The response here is one that indicates that the situation is flowing with the Tao of its nature. Most everything, at this time, seems to be in its proper place and interacting well. It is a fortuitous phase for the consultee.

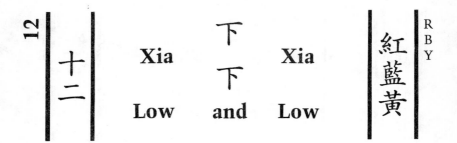

EXPLANATION: The casting results in Blue following Red. Wood cannot start fire. Good material is wasted. Yellow follows Blue. The earth is broken by wood. Fine ambitions fall apart. This is the destiny of this casting. Disaster may be avoided if one can find the way and means of retreating and for the time be content.

JUDGMENT: Wealth is hopeless. Seeking will not be at all promising. The fated times are against you. No one will recognize or aid you. The superior person will be adaptable to poverty. Do not blame heaven or one's fellows. It will only bring more suffering.

COMMENTARY: Here is a situation where the expenditure of energy has preceded the event. It is like exhausting oneself applauding the announcement of a celebrity, so that when they appear, one has no energy to participate in the applause of general approval, approbation, and enthusiastic enjoyment. No one can help you applaud, and many will look askance at you. Who can you blame? To try to blame only makes for greater discomfort. Accept that you have "blown it." This frees you for new involvements.

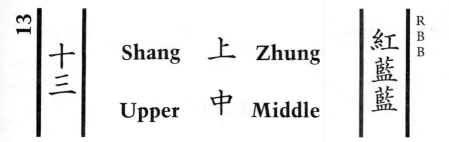

13

Shang 上 **Zhung**

Upper 中 **Middle**

紅
藍
藍

R
B
B

EXPLANATION: Two Blues follow Red in this casting. The sequence doesn't allow the woods to give rise to fire. However, the vital energies of wood are strong. The image is: woods of summer can give welcome shades, and one does not fear the hot sun above. The consultee can be self-sufficient throughout life, with no concern or worry.

JUDGMENT: Affluence will be adequate. One will be able to live with reasonable ease. However, if one becomes greedy and begins looking and plotting for riches inappropriately, it will attract much trouble, and one will become ensnarled in difficulties.

COMMENTARY: It appears that, for the time, one is inside the perimeters of a secure fate. Examine your situation carefully and evaluate it with meticulous thoroughness. It is very important for experiencing happiness that recognition be given to one's limitations. One cannot carry a gallon in a pint container.

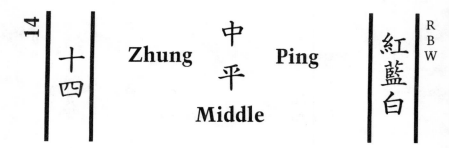

EXPLANATION: This casting places Blue following Red. No generation takes place. White following Blue implies no overcoming either. If one knows how to proceed, he will first retreat, then advance. In this way some opportunity may be found.

JUDGMENT: There may be a little affluence, but it must be pursued properly and with flexibility. The sum evaluation of the situation at this time is that there are only small opportunities possible. In general, the promise is for nothing greatly good or bad.

COMMENTARY: The components comprising the present conditions are not suitable for attaining great goals. It is like trying to collect a thousand dollars when only pennies are available. The time and effort required to collect, count, and package a thousand dollars in pennies subtracts from the full value. One should wait until money of a larger denomination is available. It is easier and quicker to collect a thousand dollars in hundred dollar bills.

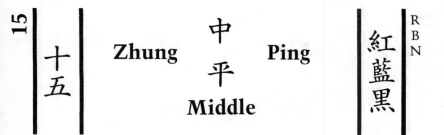

15 十五 Zhung 中平 Ping Middle 紅藍黑 R B N

EXPLANATION: The ordering of Red, Blue, and Black reverses their generating sequence. Wood cannot generate fire, and water cannot generate wood. Thus going backward would be favorable, but not advancing. One should go back and retire. Yet the sun shines on vegetation, and water flows by. The circumstances will end well, and there will be no want.

JUDGMENT: Wealth may be sought, but the ways are not smooth. To venture out, there will be gains and losses. What can be obtained will not come up to what is sought. Better return home and find other ways.

COMMENTARY: The opportunities afforded by the present situation are outweighed by the dangers and expenses of trying to avoid losses and failure. One will find greater security in retreating and waiting. There is nothing to be gained by laying supporting crossbeams for a house that have to rest upon cracked and crumbling foundation stones.

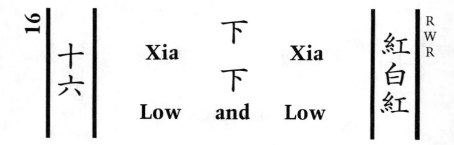

EXPLANATION: White occurs between two Reds. Fire overcomes metal. Metal meets more fire. Thus there is an image of charred rocks and melted metal. If the consultee ventures out to trade, the venture will be in vain. There will be no one to protect and assist you, and there is the prospect of loss.

JUDGMENT: Fates are unfavorable. Do not seek rashly. Any undertaking will fail. Isolated and without help, some will oppress you. Such times are to be feared.

COMMENTARY: The indications here are either: That which is being sought or considered has not been thoroughly thought through, researched, and planned; or it is an untenable project. One should abandon any further consideration of it and direct one's energies and mind to a new and different concern.

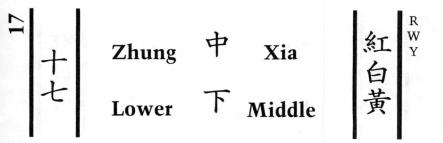

EXPLANATION: White following Red is fire overcoming metal, but here it symbolizes a pink trap drawing off one's gold. Yellow follows White. The generative powers of earth are thwarted. But if one can check one's course and return, then the power of earth to produce metal can still be restored.

JUDGMENT: Romantic entanglement. Self-checking necessary. If present desires are not controlled and one continues to pursue recklessly, there will be only harm and no benefits.

COMMENTARY: Here one has allowed the deep feelings of the heart to play too strong a role in determining one's involvement. It is urgent that the consultee reexamine the background and present status of the situation. Just because one is a canoe enthusiast, it does not mean one should excitedly paddle over the Niagara Falls.

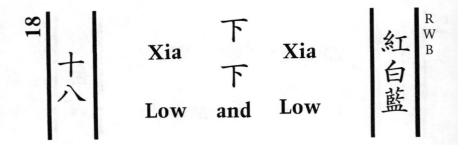

EXPLANATION: The cast has Red followed by White, and then White followed by Blue. This is fire overcoming metal and metal overcoming wood. Double overcoming. The image is like a leaking house meeting rain, a delayed boat against the wind. The times are bad. Be content in your place and do not blame the heavens.

JUDGMENT: Times are bad. All things are blocked. If you seek wealth, you receive disaster. In such times, nothing will accord with your wishes. The only recourse is to inspect yourself and cultivate your virtues. One must wait till the clouds clear in the future.

COMMENTARY: The insight here is that the situation and time are more or less completely enveloped in negativity. No effort can break through the conditions as they are at the present. The only hopeful thing to do is meditate introspectively and develop one's positive nature. In this way, when conditions and circumstances are changed and the clouds have passed on, you will meet new opportunities with fresh, vital energy.

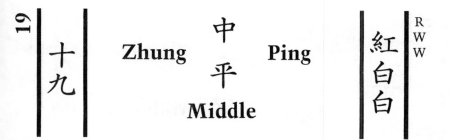

EXPLANATION: Where White follows Red, fire can overcome metal. However, here the White is doubled, thus metal is not merely overcome, but rather also refined. The blade of the sword shines out of the furnace. Although great hardship and effort had to be endured, one should note that steel is refined from crude iron.

JUDGMENT: The search for wealth has no immediate hope. But after much hardship and effort has been endured, there will be prospects of flourishing in the future. Thus do not be discouraged by present difficulties.

COMMENTARY: The present involvement seems most discouraging. But the intuitive forces that initiated your present involvement did so because of cosmic evolution. While many difficulties and setbacks attend the present situation, there is a transformation in the making that will produce strength and prosperity.

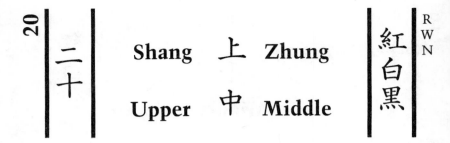

EXPLANATION: White follows Red. Fire overcomes metal. Black follows White. Metal generates water. Here the indications are that disaster turns to good fortune and success follows failure.

JUDGMENT: At first there is difficulty in the present pursuit of wealth. Later one will obtain the goal. Therefore be especially careful about careless and brash moves. Proceed calmly and wait for the coming of peace after stagnation. There will be profit and good fortune. If other questions are asked, the turn of bad fortune into good fortune can also be expected.

COMMENTARY: The situation seems impotent at the present time. However, by exercising artful speech and maneuvering with tactful skills, carefully and unobtrusively, one can eventually reap gains from the situation. It can become the stepping-stone to new successes.

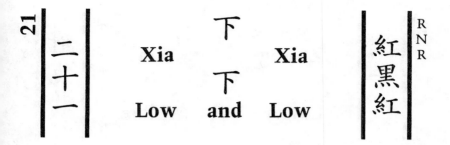

EXPLANATION: Two Reds hold one Black in the middle. Water overcomes fire, but the fire above cannot be overcome. Two antagonistic sides confront each other like two goats with horns locked. Great misfortune. The only thing to do is to cultivate one's virtues and try to avoid the situation.

JUDGMENT: These are evil times. If one is very careful, perhaps disaster may be avoided. You may lose all personal freedom. How can you seek wealth?

COMMENTARY: The consultee is in the midst of a barren and unproductive time. Efforts to advance are blocked and retreat is stopped by having burned one's bridges behind one. When confronted with the inevitable, one must accept it. Only by accepting the inevitable can one hope to be ready for the new change that must follow when the period of bad times has exhausted itself.

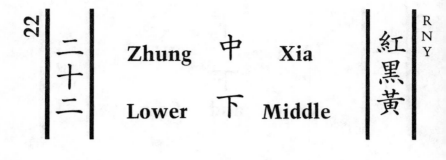

二十二　Zhung　中　Xia

Lower　下　Middle

R N Y

紅黑黃

EXPLANATION: In casting Red, Black, and Yellow in the forward sequence, they do not affect each other much. But in reverse, there will be a double overcoming. That is, earth will check water, and water will destroy fire. The consultee should struggle forward alone. But it is important, at the same time, to avoid opposing other people's tendencies. The course of events must be allowed to proceed even when there are no advantages apparent.

JUDGMENT: Good fortunes are not here. Do not pursue your goal recklessly. All affairs must be allowed to develop. This may enable the coming of peaceful days ahead. Attempts to reverse by overstepping normal bounds will bring disaster.

COMMENTARY: The situation and involvement occurs at an inauspicious time. One will not make a fortune here. All things must be allowed their development. In time, the circumstances will change and harmony will be able to manifest between situations, time, and persons.

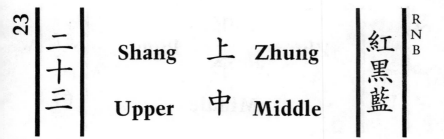

EXPLANATION: Since Red precedes Black, water does not overcome fire. Then Blue follows Black, wood is generated by water. The image is of vegetation nourished by water with the sun above. Flourishing fortune is indicated after midday. The family, especially, will prosper.

JUDGMENT: Good fortunes have arrived. What is sought will be gained. From now on, the family fortunes will turn upward. This can be predicted.

COMMENTARY: The situation is in an agreeable time, and there is an abundance of nourishment available. The time is especially propitious for increases in family good fortune. Family is not only persons, but things and ideas in close alliance.

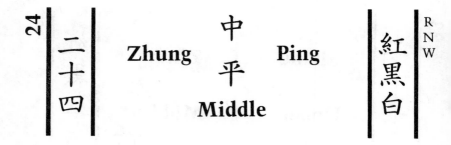

EXPLANATION: Red, Black, and White is a sequence in which the colors neither produce nor overcome each other. Even and uneventful. The image is red flower petals floating over black water, where a few goldfish swim. You may catch a few. Be content.

JUDGMENT: There is some prospect for attaining wealth, but don't be greedy and waste your wishes. Be industrious and sincere, there will be sufficient means. Perhaps matters will improve.

COMMENTARY: The situation is in a state of static balance. This means that it isn't immobile, but merely not moving much in any direction. There will be no great losses and no great gains. It is like walking from one end of a seesaw to the other—at either end you'll be able to reach no higher than you could from the other end. To attempt to jump up so as to extend one's reach invites disaster.

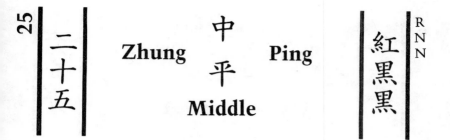

EXPLANATION: The casting that results in one Red preceding two Blacks depicts water that cannot overcome fire. The image is the sun above while dark clouds below are giving abundant rain. This is welcomed by the farmer. It is a metaphor that portends transformation of bad fortune to good fortune.

JUDGMENT: While the fates are stolidly even, with industrious effort some wealth may be obtained to fulfill one's daily wishes. But if one fears difficulty, is lazy and backward, the chances may be missed, and it will be piteous.

COMMENTARY: With intuitive insight, one is able to see beyond the dark clouds that are releasing the rain of events that inhibit your going out and moving about. Yet if your nature, like that of a farmer, is to do and grow things, these present conditions will be welcomed. The time can be used to prepare industriously for the necessary tasks to be done until the clouds pass and the sun again shines down.

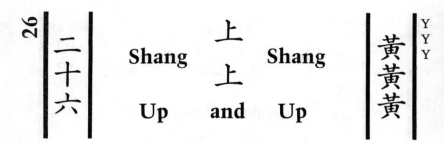

EXPLANATION: With three Yellows in a row, the power of the earth is great indeed. Great joy and good fortune. All things are nourished and sustained. The consultee has received well from the ancestor and will leave sustained wealth for the descendants. Good fortune without end.

JUDGMENT: Long lasting wealth and prosperity. Heavens respond to cultivated virtue. Portends good fortune, longevity and many descendants.

COMMENTARY: The text assigned this image is indeed euphoric. A superficial reading of it, however, may miss the deeper implications, which are indeed desirable. The phrase "has received well from the ancestor" refers not alone to financial and/or property gains, but to the examples, the teachings, and the heritage in a much broader sense. "Ancestor" is not necessarily a reference to a blood relative, but to that which preceded. After all, there is a popular belief among many people that we all are descended from a common ancestor.

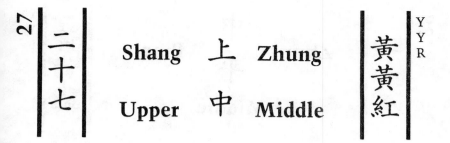

二十七

Shang 上 Zhung

Upper 中 Middle

Y Y R

黄黄紅

EXPLANATION: Two Yellows followed by one Red indicates that the power of fire is in the wrong position to generate earth. But the powers of earth are great which always sustain and nourish. And the power of fire comes late, which indicates flourishing in the autumn season.

JUDGMENT: Affluence will develop around the ninth and tenth moons. Do not be impatient even though the beginnings may not be as one wishes. Do not despair. Move when the time arrives. Things will certainly flourish.

COMMENTARY: Each thing manifests in its season. Good fortune is no exception to this axiom. Efforts have been great and the desire is strong; together they generate a degree of anxiety. At this time one is in a situation very much like that of a farmer who has cleared some very difficult land, and painfully tilled it, and planted his seeds. There has been so much activity prior to now that the waiting for the seeds to germinate and show signs of development produces a great anxiety. Be patient. When the right things have been done before, the right things must follow.

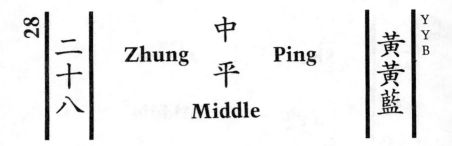

EXPLANATION: When Blue follows two Yellows, wood is not in the position to overcome earth. Rather the thickness of the earth supports the wood. Therefore cultivate industriously. Remain with your task. Continue to advance, lest you fail just before success.

JUDGMENT: What affluence is destined here must be obtained through industrious cultivation. Be thrifty and persevering. If quick results are sought and efforts are not complete, all will be of no avail.

COMMENTARY: Impatience and the feeling that one "is entitled" can endanger the prospects for attainment. Just drawing plans will not erect a building. Just planting seeds will not ensure their growth. One must collect and assemble the materials designated in the plans and one must build. One must irrigate and weed the soil where seeds are planted to cause them to grow. Blueprints are useless and planting seeds futile when the follow-through effort is not complete.

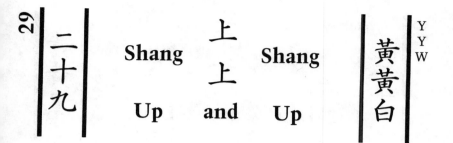

EXPLANATION: The casting is two Yellows followed by one White. It symbolizes the strong and steady powers of earth producing gold. Great fortune has been slowly accumulated as in the cultivation of virtue.

JUDGMENT: The fates are prosperous. Good fortune comes from heaven. Cultivation of virtue has been rewarded. It is not merely luck. In conducting business, often slow accumulations can become great riches and establish a good foundation for the children.

COMMENTARY: Fate is different from nature. It is the nature of a bull to have four legs, a tail, and horns. That it may have a ring through its nose is its fate. Fate is the constantly changing summation of the handling of experience. When events encircle us, the way in which we hold to the center and handle them determines what we will experience immediately and eventually. Being aware of this enables you to lay foundations for future affluence.

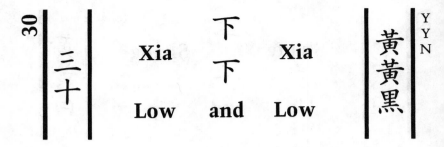

三十

Xia

下
下

Xia

Low and Low

黃
黃
黑

Y Y
N

EXPLANATION: This cast gives one Black following two Yellows. Double earth overcomes water. The image is tall mountains, narrow road, and obstructions in the river. Better exercise great care in everything. Ways of the world are difficult and full of danger. Pass your days in contented reserve. In this manner, you may avoid the calamities of the time.

JUDGMENT: Times are unfavorable. Affluence is not possible. Difficulties and obstructions stand in the way. If these words are not heeded, disaster will fall heavily.

COMMENTARY: The synchronistic reflection here is one that perceives a whirlpool of antitheses. One seems to be equipped with many things, none of which are correct or proper for the need at hand. It is as if one on a journey manages to purchase a wagon just before coming to a river where one will need a boat, then later finds a life raft at the foot of a high mountain. For the time being, find a way to be content with where you are until circumstances and conditions change.

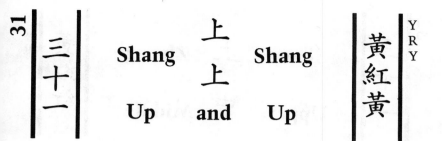

Shang 上上 **Shang**

Up and **Up**

Y
R
Y

黄
紅
黄

EXPLANATION: Casting one Red between two Yellows indicates fire generating earth backward and forward. The image is buried treasure in the earth revealing itself. Glowing fortunes are here.

JUDGMENT: Affluence is evident. Wealth and plenty are immediate. Go and claim it from the southeast. There is certainty of obtaining the prize.

COMMENTARY: The conditions are very favorable at this time. You are, by all indications, well equipped and well regarded, so that your claim upon success will not be disputed. Your movement and pace should be guided by the meaning of 135 degrees. Now is the time to complete your plans.

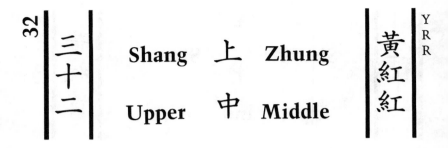

32

三十二 Shang 上 Zhung

Upper 中 Middle

黄 Y R
紅 R
紅

EXPLANATION: Yellow followed by two Reds. While fire does not generate earth in this sequence, it is doubled and flourishing. The combination is harmonious and mutually supportive. The image indicates happy enjoyments of spring and returning with honor. Good news comes in the second moon.

JUDGMENT: Wealth is coming, mainly during the second moon. Satisfaction with the breath of spring (romance), is indicated. One returns with the prize even the youth will envy. The means of advancing need not be elaborated; only the joy of honorable return is predicted.

COMMENTARY: The consultee is in an environment that contains everything that is necessary for a comfortable and enjoyable life. When one makes the effort to gain it, one will be rewarded. Great articulations and gaudy facades are not required. More is to be gained by honest modesty than braggadocio.

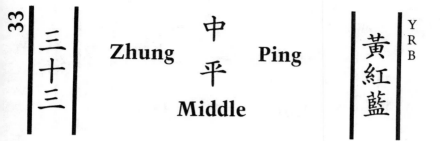

33

三十三

Zhung 中平 **Ping**

Middle

黄紅藍

Y
R
B

EXPLANATION: The Yellow, Red, and Blue cast structures the generative sequence in reverse. Wood does not produce fire, and fire does not produce earth. Thinking back, one remembers better times. The present course does not proceed well. But if one can survey the situation without ambitions, though the spring blossoms are gone, the summer woods remain, and there is peace and leisure still in the shade of the trees.

JUDGMENT: The time for wealth has passed. Now one may only guard what remains. There may be small hopes, but there will be no prosperity as in the past. Cultivate your virtues and rest in self-sufficiency. Do not waste lamentations on bygone days.

COMMENTARY: Opportunities for gaining wealth and acquiring affluence have subsided. The small glimmerings one may be hoping in should be recognized as the after-vibrations of previously enjoyed abundance, and not the promise of new fulfillments. One can avoid pain and despondency by settling into the requirements of self-sufficiency and turning to the meditative cultivation of one's virtues.

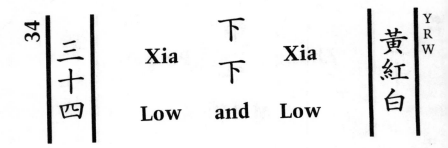

EXPLANATION: Casting so that Red follows Yellow indicates that fire does not generate earth. White following Red pictures fire overcoming metal. The image is the road ends. The sun sets. Money is exhausted. Returning empty-handed, one can only wait for a better future.

JUDGMENT: Times are not supportive. Fate is not kind. Not only is there no hope for gain, there is fear of loss. To venture out is bound to end in failure. It is better to stay put and remain on guard.

COMMENTARY: This is a depressing interlude, and any attempts to make gain out of it are doomed. The very best that can be accomplished at this time is to remain very alert. Do not venture into schemes directed at making a profit, as they cannot succeed at this time. Study minutely the nature of your present predicament. In this way, you will come to recognize where and when it weakens. Then you can break through and take advantage of new conditions.

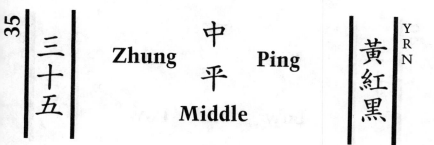

三十五 | Zhung 中平 Ping Middle | 黄红黑 | Y R N

EXPLANATION: In this casting, Red follows Yellow, fire does not produce earth. Black follows Red, water does not destroy fire. Neither generating nor overcoming takes place. This indicates neither gain nor loss. But since there is no loss, simple industry will sustain us. Plain food and clothes. What worries are there?

JUDGMENT: The fates are uneventful. Not much hope for wealth. But there is sufficiency for life. Do not have wild thoughts. They bring only vexations.

COMMENTARY: In your personal life this is a period of mediocrity. The greatest comfort can be experienced by accepting and using wisely the sufficiencies that are at hand. Ambitious speculation and unbridled efforts to make great gains at this time will result in anguish.

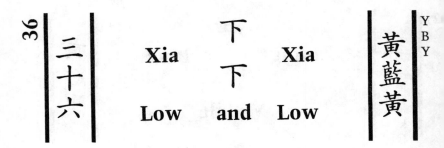

EXPLANATION: Blue between two Yellows. Wood between earth. Destructive influence backward and forward. In this situation, while wood breaks up earth, wood is itself buried. This yields the image of leaves turning yellow and good material covered by earth. One's fate is stagnated. Good talents are unrecognized. A sad situation.

JUDGMENT: The times are "splitting apart" and there is no "return." Placed beneath others, unrecognized by any, good talents are wasted. Whatever is sought at this time, there will be nothing gained. Better remain home and wait for the time of "return."

COMMENTARY: You seem to be in the midst of strong negative influences. Projects are not apt to develop well. Those things that are most strongly desired are best not striven for at this time. It is important to wait until the return of harmonious conditions.

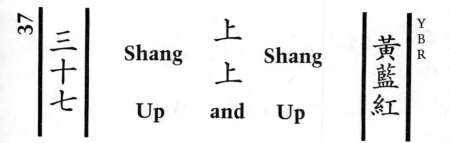

EXPLANATION: This casting gives a generating sequence all the way. Blue follows Yellow and Red follows Blue. The image: out of luxuriant but dark woods in the mountains one emerges upon another valley bright with flowers. The consultee is with the times. Advance is favorable. One may proceed with diligence. One will meet with good fortune.

JUDGMENT: Times are right. Advance quickly without tiring. Unexpected wealth will be in store. The future is far-reaching. By chance one may be helped by the great. Do not miss the opportunity.

COMMENTARY: You are presently in the midst of propitious conditions. Many doors are opening. There are chances of being helped by a number of influential persons in a number of avenues you wish to pursue. Selectivity is important during a time of abundance. For what is selected will become a strong factor in determining what the future will be.

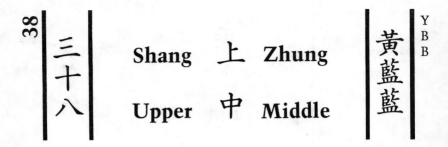

三十八　Shang 上 Zhung

Upper 中 Middle

YBB

黄藍藍

EXPLANATION: When the cast forms one Yellow preceding two Blues, the power of wood is not directed to earth; therefore it does not overcome earth. Rather in this case, the earth sustains wood, and wood flourishes doubly. Wood is east. It is spring. It is *chen*, thunder. Thunder sounds spring is here. Good fortune is to be found in the east.

JUDGMENT: Affluence increases. Wealth and good fortune will flourish in the spring. Seek for them in the east. Whether opening a store, conducting business, or going on a trip, aiming eastward will certainly bring great profit.

COMMENTARY: You are within the perimeters of vibrations of plentitude. "Good fortune is to be found in the east" means that this is an excellent time to become involved in something new, young, or something that is renewed. One should apply this counsel in the very broadest manner in order to profit from it most advantageously. Look beyond the words to the phenomenal process imaged by the sense of the words.

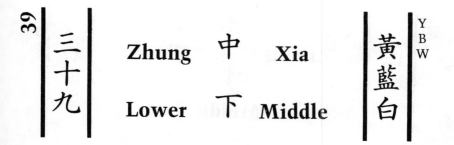

EXPLANATION: This casting that constructs the sequence of Yellow, Blue, and White seems apparently harmless. But if one looks backward, it will be seen that metal is destructive to wood and wood is destructive to earth. Therefore, while there are no obstructions going forward, to look back will be trouble.

JUDGMENT: For wealth it is not yet the time. Only try not to do anything upside down. Follow the proper path, step by step, and you will not be troubled. That is already lucky.

COMMENTARY: The situation, while not firm, is nevertheless tenable. By careful adherence to the permissible and impermissible, you can avoid disagreeableness and loss. On occasions of stress, do not call attention to past incidents to mitigate present mistakes. All hopes for a fortuitous culmination rest upon giving the proper corrective action to matters at hand.

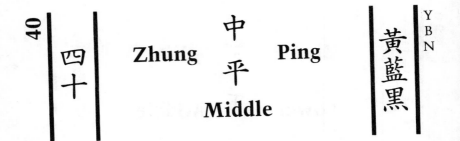

40 四十 Zhung 中平 Ping Middle 黄藍黑 YBN

EXPLANATION: Blue follows Yellow, wood does not overcome earth. Black follows Blue, water does not produce wood. No danger and no benefits. The image is the fisherman in a boat drinking wine in the evening. The times are serene but the joys are illusory.

JUDGMENT: Prospects for wealth only fair. What can be gained will not satisfy the need. But there are no constraints and pressures. One may feel carefree. As the book says, "knowing contentment there will be no disgrace."

COMMENTARY: The situation appears to be placid. By not striving to exceed one's capabilities, one can avoid loss. At the time, there are no extreme pressures from circumstances or persons requiring undo effort. Rest from arduous activity and enjoy the interlude as a vacation.

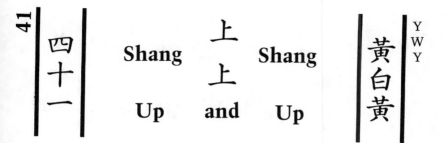

EXPLANATION: White between two Yellows. This cast pictures earth producing metal with more production promised. The image is gold in the earth. Great profit. One will chance upon guidance. No laborious search necessary.

JUDGMENT: Wealth and fortune certain. The time of discovery has arrived. Someone will point out the location. Great profit. A chance meeting will be most fortunate.

COMMENTARY: The likelihood is very great that you will be approached by someone with an offer that will be very advantageous for you. Pointing out the location refers not exclusively to a geographical spot, but also to the area of pursuit wherein great advance and profit await you.

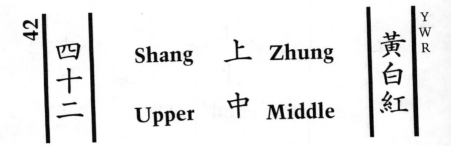

四十二 | Shang 上 Zhung

Upper 中 Middle

黄白紅 Y W R

EXPLANATION: White following Yellow is earth producing metal. Red following White is fire not overcoming metal. The image for the present is that the production of wealth has been done in the proper way, that is, with a good heart. Thus a good inheritance will be left to the children.

JUDGMENT: The present fortunes for wealth are long lasting. It is favorable to conduct legitimate business. Always be fair and guard your reputation. Then a good foundation will be established for your descendants. Cultivate virtue and you will be rewarded. This is so from ancient times.

COMMENTARY: The time is conspicuously favorable for you. By giving attention to the commonplace amenities and exercising caution, one secures and extends the good fortune inherent in the present time.

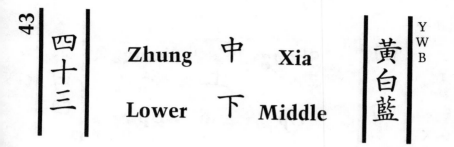

EXPLANATION: White follows Yellow is earth producing metal. But blue follows White is metal overcoming wood. In imagery, one is reminded that to lose a horse may not be a calamity, nor gaining a horse good fortune. The book says: "bad fortune is what good fortune leans on, good fortune is what bad fortune hides in."

JUDGMENT: Wealth and fortune come and go. They do not last. "First laughter then tears." "Curses and blessings do not come through gates, but man himself invites their arrival." Think about these sayings.

COMMENTARY: Affluence is a variable commodity. No matter how long one has been engaged in accumulating it and no matter how great it is, it can disappear in a flashing moment. Keep in mind that today's merriment will be tomorrow's sad nostalgia.

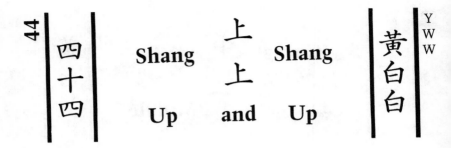

EXPLANATION: Here two Whites follow Yellow. Earth generates gold. Power of gold is doubled. Thus, in imagery, one may speak of gold found in sand and jade revealed in rock. Seek wealth and wealth is obtained. All matters develop according to one's wish. Much to be congratulated.

JUDGMENT: Fortune and wealth flourish greatly. What is sought will be obtained. Specially favorable to industry where the profits will be even greater.

COMMENTARY: This is an excellent time to exert one's energies to the task of attaining long-desired goals. These goals may be financial, academic, or romantic. "Specially favorable to industry" does not refer only to business. The broader meaning is that any intensified exercise directed toward a target will be even the more generously rewarded.

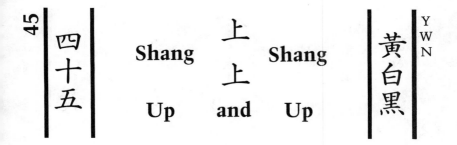

EXPLANATION: White following Yellow is earth generating metal. Black following White is metal generating water. The image is stone containing jade and water harboring pearls. The time has come for the consultee. Smooth sailing. All welcome him and admire his glory.

JUDGMENT: Fortune flourishes as a blazing fire. There is immediate prospect of gaining the prize. All things will be smooth and without obstructions. In whatever business there will be a full return.

COMMENTARY: The situation and conditions of the moment are strongly conducive to great success. However, it is well to remember that though a gold nugget may lie at one's foot, one remains just that much poorer if one will not stoop to pick it up. All of the blessings of fate will be of no avail if one does not perform in a manner that begets honor, respect, and support.

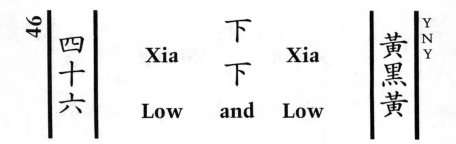

EXPLANATION: When the cast comes out a Black between two Yellows, it symbolizes water checked by earth forward and backward. Neither advance nor retreat is possible. It portends great misfortune. Turn your whole mind toward goodness. Perhaps the danger can be escaped.

JUDGMENT: It is a time of misfortune. Do not ask about wealth. There is danger all around. No road is open for advance or retreat. Forget yourself and concentrate on good deeds. This is one way to escape danger.

COMMENTARY: The situation is without merit, and the conditions surrounding it hold nothing that can in any way alleviate the prospects of misfortune. There is no way open to return to a time of better practices. There is no means of projecting new policies that promise a fresh growth in the future. All is negative. The counsel is intelligent and good. Concentrate on doing good deeds. This alone may protect you from deadening disaster.

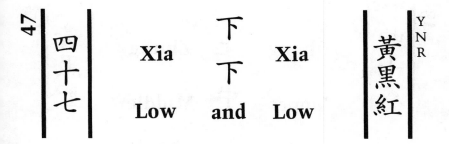

EXPLANATION: Where the cast puts Yellow followed by Black, the earth is overcoming water. Black followed by Red is water overcoming fire. Overcoming repeated. The image is one confronted by a mountain that is hard to cross and a river that is hard to ford. It is a dark night without the moon. Be still. Perhaps you will not fall.

JUDGMENT: Fate is dark. Times are full of obstructions. Retreat and be on guard so as not to lose your footing. If you are reckless and continue to search for wealth, there will be calamity.

COMMENTARY: Why are you asking about this matter? You are fully aware that it is tightly laced with dangers. It is purposeless to paint a canvas black in a blackened room. Return to old values and concentrate upon developing your internal virtues. Thus you can avoid the anguish and pain of despondency.

101

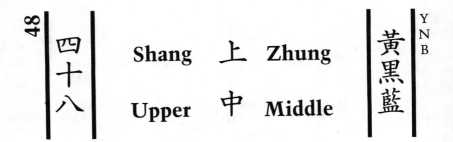

四十八　48　Shang 上 Zhung　Upper 中 Middle　黃黑藍 YNB

EXPLANATION:　Yellow followed by Black is earth overcoming water. But Black followed by Blue is water generating wood. The image: If the cold seasons are endured, renewed flourishing comes later as the pine and cedar. The consultee will find first bitterness, then sweet. Good fortune comes in the late years.

JUDGMENT:　Fortunes are first obstructed then smooth. No immediate prospects. Must wait till end of winter and the return of spring. Then there is great hope. A person should have contentment in poverty and be able to endure. Do not lose hope or will.

COMMENTARY:　The going is presently rough. The outlook is not promising at the moment. It is winter in the cycle of fortune. Hold on to your ideals and to the matter in hand. By waiting for the proper time, you will display remarkable stamina that begets you voluntary help when you will need it much later on.

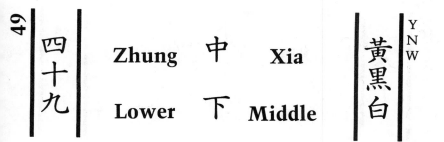

49

四十九

Zhung 中 Xia

Lower 下 Middle

黄黑白

Y
N
W

EXPLANATION: Black follows Yellow. Water overcomes earth. Conflict and hostility is implied. Therefore an image of birds and beasts not belonging together. White follows Black, nothing happens. Metal could be produced by earth, but water stands in the way. The way cannot be practiced. One thinks of going home. The consultee should return.

JUDGMENT: Fate and fortune are not smooth. Be careful making friends. Venturing out, be on guard against deception and entrapment. Human hearts can be treacherous. Better return to your home and plan for other endeavors.

COMMENTARY: The indication here is one of complicated and irreconcilable elements. Things and people do not seem to fit together well. Understanding and sympathy is not attainable. Extreme caution must be exercised before putting your trust in others. This is the meaning of the phrase "human hearts can be treacherous."

103

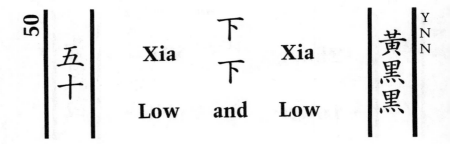

EXPLANATION: Two blacks follow Yellow. Earth overcomes water. Here waters are in flood, only barely kept in check, but the image points up another aspect: "the ocean of misery is endless, but the shore is just behind." Please observe the teaching.

JUDGMENT: Bad times are not over. Do not envy the wealth of others and cherish vain illusions. If some small gains are achieved, they will also bring misfortune. Better do some honest work and patiently wait for the times to change.

COMMENTARY: You are in the midst of tough and critical situations. It is important to hold to ethical and moral principles. Do not allow yourself to be diverted from correct paths by the glitter of another's possessions. They may not be as genuine as you imagine. The present time is best spent in simple ventures, self-improvement studies, and patient calculated inaction.

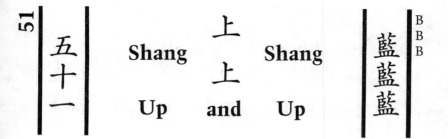

五十一　Shang　上上　Shang
　　　　　Up　and　Up　　藍藍藍　B B B

EXPLANATION: To cast three Blues together indicates that the power of wood is full indeed. Follow the commands of spring (lunar commands). The ten thousand things are flourishing. The consultee is enjoying the time of peace. Further there is help from someone in high position. Prosperity all the way.

JUDGMENT: Wealth and fortune flourish in the spring. Prosperity flourishes in the east. What is sought will be achieved. Fame and fortune both will be yours. Be it in conducting business, transporting goods, doing construction, starting industry, all will flourish. Portends great good fortune.

COMMENTARY: The color Blue represents wood. Wood is equated with solidity and comparative ease in workability. This gives an image of "togetherness" in heaven, earth, and man, that is suited to being developed in any chosen direction or manner. But what is selected to be pursued is very important. Hence it reads, "What is sought will be achieved. Fame and fortune both will be yours." What is sought is not a verbal declaration or a wished for thing, but rather what we put our interest and energies into.

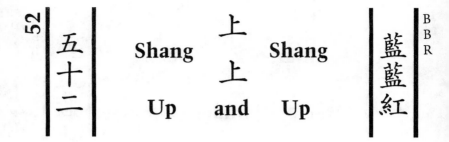

EXPLANATION: One Red follows two Blue, flourishing wood generating fire. The image is the plum blossom, the first of the flowers in the spring. The time has come for the consultee. In all business, you will exceed others.

JUDGMENT: The way is open for fortune and wealth. Great flourishing from winter to spring. You may occupy the lead and not be second to anyone. But whether trading goods or achieving honors, you must hasten forward and grasp quickly lest others surpass you.

COMMENTARY: The opportunities which are now available to you must be taken advantage of immediately. This is a time of great promise, but like plum blossoms, which are among the earliest to bloom in the spring, they do not last long. Use your intuitive sensitivity to make the most timely decisions. To hesitate will permit others to overtake and surpass you.

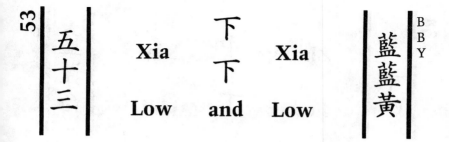

EXPLANATION: Two Blues preceding one Yellow. Weight of twice wood overcoming one earth. The image indicates overwhelming pressure, especially when the foundations are weak. Your roots are lowly and the fates are heavy.

JUDGMENT: Destiny shallow, fortunes obstructed. You are oppressed by others. There is no hope yet for deliverance. In such circumstances, the only thing to do is to make firm one's own standing. Uproot faults and plant virtue, endure to the best of one's ability. Do not fuss and complain, it will only bring insults and disgrace.

COMMENTARY: It has been said by Robert Browning, a man's reach should exceed his grasp, or what's a heaven for?" But when a man's arm is in a sling, then reaching itself is not possible. The present conditions do not allow you to exercise your full talents. To attempt to do so will only compound difficulties and cause you to appear foolish before others. Ambition, when unbridled, can be a fault. Uproot faults and develop virtues.

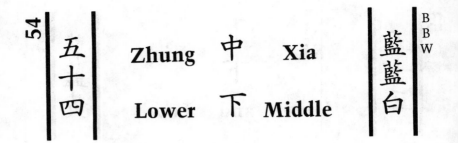

54 五十四 Zhung 中 Xia Lower 下 Middle B B W 藍藍白

EXPLANATION: One White follows two Blues. While metal is not in a position to overcome wood, their relationship is not good. The power of wood is strong, but it has come to an end. The image is good autumn days, but the evening sun is setting. There may be some good fortune in the late years, but the years will not last.

JUDGMENT: There is some hope for wealth in the late fall. But soon after it will be over. To receive this judgment in one's late years means there may be a few good years left.

COMMENTARY: The references to autumn and late fall convey several meanings. It may refer to the literal autumn season when good fortune can be expected. It can be referring to the latter part of a project. Good fortune is to be expected when the project nears completion. Again it indicates that the consultee will have some small good fortune in the later years of his life.

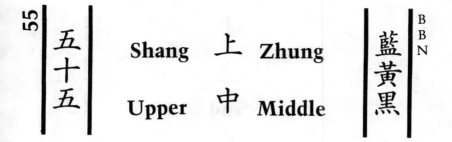

五十五

Shang 上 Zhung

Upper 中 Middle

藍黃黑

B B N

EXPLANATION: To cast so that one Black follows two Blues puts water in a position so that it does not generate wood, but the relationship is supportive. The image is a river flowing by the woods. In this position, there comes someone to point the way. Good fortune will be reached.

JUDGMENT: The way to fortune is open. There is hope for wealth. Once someone in a high position extends his help, you will be able to pass into a happier realm. If you are seeking for this opportunity, go toward the northeast.

COMMENTARY: The indication here is that something of value will be found in what seems to be a barren area. However, a new beginning is possible just at the time and in the place you think least promising.

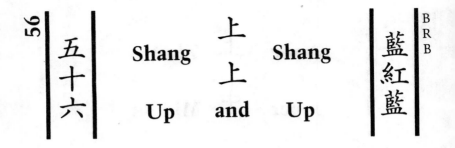

五十六 Shang 上上 Shang Up and Up 藍紅藍 B R B

EXPLANATION: One Red between two Blues. Wood generating fire backward and forward. Five rises. Red and Blue yields purple light. The image is climbing the tower to view the morning sun rising in the east. The consultee's fortunes are flourishing in the extreme. For starting a family and establishing a business, this is just the time.

JUDGMENT: Fortune and wealth are here as the rising sun. The views are broad, the prospects are wide. Whether in art, business, or industry, your fame will go around the world. Profits will be a thousandfold. Great happiness.

COMMENTARY: This is such an excellent casting that it is important to have an expansive understanding of it. Good fortune is rising like the sun, revealing broad perspectives of opportunities to choose from. At this time you may select a number of goals, and you will gain an enviable success in them.

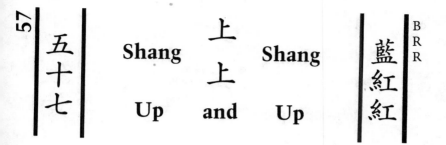

五
十
七

Shang 上 **Shang**
上

Up and **Up**

藍
紅
紅

B
R
R

EXPLANATION: Here one Blue is followed by two Reds. One wood generating double fire. The image indicates the temperature in the furnace is right, and the pill of immortality has completed its nine circuits. All are ready. Good results may be expected for all undertakings.

JUDGMENT: Fortune has reached the point of peace. Star of wealth shines bright. Energies flourish. Great profit in all business. Opportunities are right. Fame and fortune may both be obtained. Good foundations may be laid for the descendants.

COMMENTARY: The phrase "Good foundations may be laid for the descendants" is intended to awaken the consciousness to the fact that even though the conditions are quite ideal for making progress and gaining wealth, the security to be realized by the gains will be determined by the degree of patience, planning and farsightedness which are put into the effort of realizing a fortune. The more one projects for the enduringness of the fortune, the more meaningful it becomes.

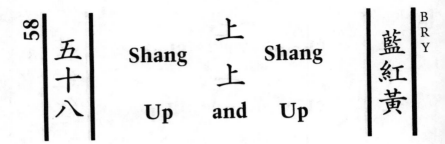

EXPLANATION: Blue followed by Red is wood generating fire. Red followed by Yellow is fire generating earth. The image is divine red fruits ripening in the blue heaven, bringing benefits to earth. This portends great good fortune.

JUDGMENT: Fortune and wealth are here. Good luck descends from heaven. Doing good deeds and cultivating virtue brings divine response. Much support from heaven, no need for human assistance. Excellence of the situation surpasses many. All this has been well deserved and did not come by mere chance.

COMMENTARY: This casting represents the cosmic forces all in a positive and generating sequence. Wood is used for generating fire, and the fire follows. The ashes which become the residue of fire represents new pure earth, free of contaminants. Earth is the medium through which the cosmic forces mysteriously manifest all forms of life. The conditions surrounding you at this time are very much like this. Past actions and relationships have set the foundations for new successes.

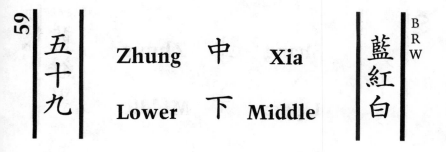

五十九   Zhung 中 Xia

Lower 下 Middle

藍紅白   B R W

EXPLANATION: When Red is followed by Blue, wood is generating fire. But Red followed by White is fire overcoming metal. The image is that the words of many can melt gold. Fame and fortune give rise to envy, jealousy, and gossip. Therefore the famous must be wary of pride. Show yourself retiring and humble, and gossip will cease.

JUDGMENT: Fortunes are flourishing. Much can be obtained. But one must not take anything unrighteously and harm others. Otherwise all gains will be in vain, and nothing will last. Therefore the ancient one (Lao Tzu) observed, "First establish virtue, then achievement."

COMMENTARY: Affluence, fortune, and reputation can be most easily dissolved by the acrid acids of envy, jealousy, and gossip. When one is secure, strong, and influential, it is wise to move timidly, strike with gentleness, and influence with the greatest possible subtlety. Adherence to the ways of justice and honesty becomes a fortress of defense against all manner of vileness.

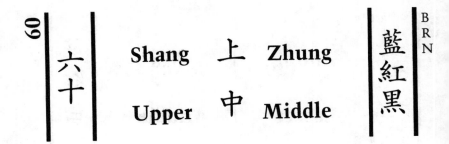

EXPLANATION: Here Blue precedes Red. Wood generates fire. Black follows Red. Fire is not harmed by water. The image is from the green field in which jade is obtained. Still one looks for pearls in the muddy water. While it is difficult to find the pearls, one must not hesitate to advance with the search. For to hesitate would be to allow water to wash back upon the fire. There is some hope for profit.

JUDGMENT: Fortunes are favorable. Some small profit is possible immediately. The larger profits are still ahead. Do not rest and do not be daunted by the difficulties, and you will be rewarded for the effort.

COMMENTARY: The present involvement offers a modest degree of security. The opportunity for greater gain is ahead. Do not be lulled by present comforts so that you withdraw from the pursuit of greater treasures. The challenge and effort to work for greater gains is demanding and filled with difficulties. Your very engagement in the "game" will stir admiration and beget reward.

114

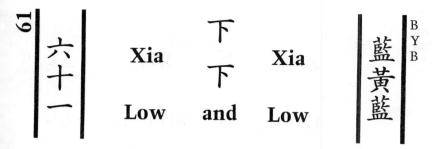

61

六十一　Xia　下下　Xia　Low and Low　藍黃藍　BYB

EXPLANATION: A Yellow is cast between two Blues. Earth is overcome by wood from both directions. The image is of a mountain path overgrown with thorns. The fate of the consultee is full of difficulties. It is not favorable to advance. If forced, the efforts are wasted. At times and in places, the ways of the world are treacherous, and harm may befall one from evil-minded men. Better return to the farm.

JUDGMENT: Fortunes are blocked. It is not favorable to advance. To use force will be of no avail. Besides, the ways of evil are deceptive and ensnaring. Retreat to the fields, some gains may be made there.

COMMENTARY: The present predicament is greatly confounding. One looks about in vain to find some means of relief. It is best to halt all action. By retreating to the farm, one will become freshly involved in an environment of new growth and nuturing. Search for new ideas. Be innovative. In the fields of meditation and inward peering, one will discover a cornucopia of unique potential waiting for expression.

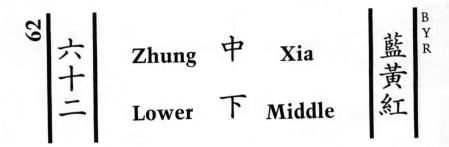

EXPLANATION: Blue followed by Yellow is wood overcoming earth. Red follows Yellow. Fire is not in the position to generate earth. The image is jade locked in the closet. The caterpillar hiding in the earth. Good materials are left unused. But once the fortunes turn, fire may perhaps receive the support of earth and stored jade may still be brought out and fetch a good price.

JUDGMENT: The present time holds no immediate hope for wealth. To seek recklessly only brings disgrace. In such times, store your wares and wait. When fortune has turned, there will be chances for profit.

COMMENTARY: The circumstances and conditions of your present position are not helpful or conducive to productivity. It may be that you have excellent ideas and are capable of good performance; but no matter how high the quality of the bricks and the perfection of the mortar mixture, one will not succeed in building a foundation in the bottom of a lake. Circumstances and conditions must complement the requirement of the structure, the materials, and the tools used. Wait until the lake has been drained or dried up. One should not attempt to build, except on solid ground.

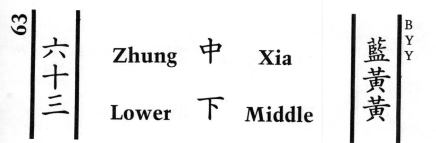

六十三

Zhung 中 Xia

Lower 下 Middle

藍黃黃

B
Y
Y

EXPLANATION: Yellow following Blue is earth overcome by wood. Wealth and fortune passes. But here the Yellow is doubled. The virtue of earth is strong. It indicates great sincerity and a generous heart. With such virtues, even calamity may be transformed into good fortune.

JUDGMENT: Wealth and fortune are not fixed through life. Much depends on the changes of your heart. Calamities and blessings are attracted by yourself. There fore, if you are seeking wealth, first rectify your heart.

COMMENTARY: Present involvements seem meager. One feels as though one is in a corral where there is no gate. Yet within this dark hopelessness, there is a glimmer of a dream. Concentrate upon the dream, thereby you become unware of the dark hopelessness. This change of heart, which is a change in view, will activate strong forces of creativity within you. You will devise a perfect means of scaling the corral of limitations. It is a universal truism: "calamities and blessings are attracted by yourself."

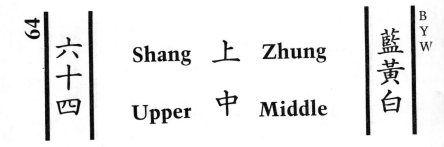

Shang 上 Zhung

Upper 中 Middle

EXPLANATION: Blue followed by Yellow is wood overcoming earth. But Yellow followed by White is earth generating metal. Fortunes are first bad, then good. The image is that when fortunes are waning, gold can lose its color; but when fortunes advance, even iron will shine. Now the future is favorable.

JUDGMENT: The pathways to fortune will open up after initial obstructions are overcome. Profit will come in the fall. All who are involved in business that has met failure should not abandon hope. From now on, not only is recovery possible, but aid will come from someone in high position, and the sailing will be smooth hereafter.

COMMENTARY: The hoped for success and gain has not measured up to expectations. One may become despondent and hyper-self-critical. These attitudes are obstructions to reaching a solution. Overcome these obstructions, and the display of courage and resolution will attract supportive endorsement and assistance from influential centers.

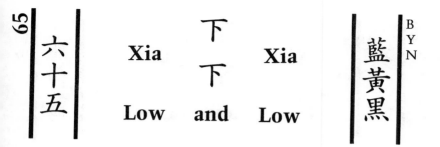

EXPLANATION: Blue followed by Yellow is wood overcoming earth. Yellow followed by Black is earth overcoming water. The image is struggling through the mountains only to be lost in the marshes. The consultee is encountering the times of "splitting apart." Retreat and find contentment within. Avoid the despair.

JUDGMENT: Achievement of wealth completely hopeless. To seek will only bring disaster. Under the circumstances, if one can only find a place of security, it is already by the greatest of luck. If one risks forward movement, the future will be unthinkable.

COMMENTARY: The present is like being high on the side of a mountain, where the mist and fog is so thick that one cannot see below to distinguish between dry land and the marshes. To struggle through the mist and fog at this time will almost surely lead one into the marshlands. It will be better to find a spot that secures you from the chill and dangers of where you are. For now, one must wait for the mist and fog to lift before attempting to move ahead.

119

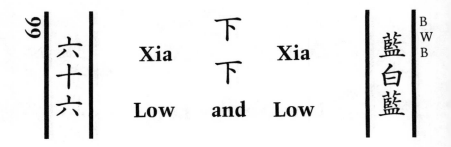

EXPLANATION: You are given one White between two Blues. Metal overcomes wood backward and forward. No freedom to move in either direction. The image is snow filling up the pass. It will be necessary to wait till the spring, when wood flourishes again, before there can be a turn of fortune.

JUDGMENT: The fates are blocked. Wealth hopeless. No way to go forward. No one will pity you. To venture out will bring many calamities. Better return and wait out the time before greater losses are encountered.

COMMENTARY: The conditions that presently surround you are greatly restrictive. There is not much choice or opportunity for self-expression or elective determination. "To wait till the spring, when wood flourishes again" means biding one's time until the fixed and frozen conditions of the present thaw out and an elasticity of new ideas and permissiveness allows for the development of new techniques to achieve desired goals.

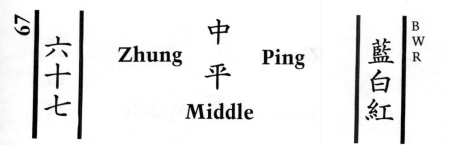

67 六十七 Zhung 中平 Ping Middle 藍白紅 B W R

EXPLANATION: Blue, White, and Red form the overcoming sequence in reverse. In this order, fire does not overcome metal, and metal does not overcome wood. This is fortunate. However, the situation is precarious since the relationships are not friendly. Therefore the image urges one to stake all and forge ahead. Possibilities lie only forward.

JUDGMENT: While the way to wealth and fortune is not very smooth, if one will strive forward with courage, there is still something to be obtained. A man's will can sometimes determine his fate.

COMMENTARY: The environment here is not harmonious, and one is apt to be functioning in an antagonistic atmosphere. Yet through persistent application of attention to the needs at hand, one can still obtain something. These are difficulties not to avoid but to overcome. Therein lies the opportunity for new beginnings and new successes.

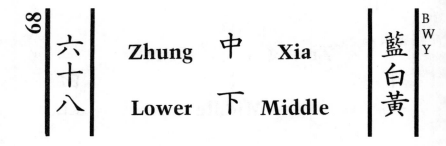

EXPLANATION: Blue precedes White. No overcoming takes place. But Yellow follows White, nothing is generated either. Between Blue and White, the relationship is hostile. No cooperation. White and Yellow reversed. No life force. Thus great treasures are buried in the earth.

JUDGMENT: Good times are not yet here. The search for wealth will be fruitless. There is no one to help. Difficult to find a friend. Fine abilities remain buried.

COMMENTARY: Within the earth, metal is produced. Earth is never produced within metal. The hostility vibrating in this situation is mostly inner-contained but nevertheless externally felt. It makes for feelings of uneasiness, but isn't overt enough to provoke active response. For this reason, the qualities and attributes you possess lie dormant and unexpressed. Seek deeper self-understanding. Your finer qualities are yet to be discovered.

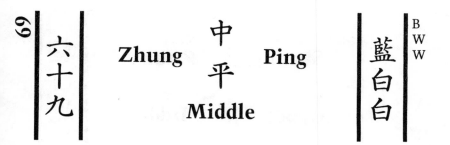

EXPLANATION: Two Whites follow one Blue. While metal does not overcome wood, their relationship remains hostile. The image is finding a rock in a thorn bush. Injuries sustained in the search. But later the rock is discovered to conceal jade. Efforts are rewarded.

JUDGMENT: Fortunes first difficult, then easy. Do not be impatient in your search for wealth. You may incur some calamities. Endure present difficulties and hold to simplicity. Opportunity will arrive later for fame and profit.

COMMENTARY: The present time is like the aiming at a target. It is difficult to correlate gravitational pull, wind velocities, and firing arc so that one can accurately hit the bull's-eye. The factors of importance and influence are so variable that perfect planning is nigh impossible. Do not let this condition discourage or dissuade you. Contending with them will strengthen you for the time of opportunity that is approaching.

123

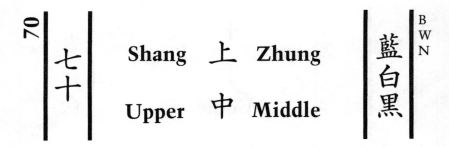

70

七十

Shang 上 Zhung

Upper 中 Middle

藍白黑 B W N

EXPLANATION: Metal does not overcome wood, as White follows Blue. Black follows White. Metal generates water. The image is a small boat sailing many lakes, then finding a pearl in the water. If the consultee is interested in carrying on a business, the opportunity will arrive. Wealth can be obtained.

JUDGMENT: The prospect for wealth is excellent. But one must enter the business world and carry on diligently. Only then may opportunities be encountered and the treasured pearl obtained.

COMMENTARY: There are happy and harmonious vibrations all about you. For some time, you have skirted about looking at this and that, here and there. At the moment, you have grasped upon a pearl. It is yet beneath the surface. You must dive in for it and bring it to the surface with conscientious dedication and persistence.

124

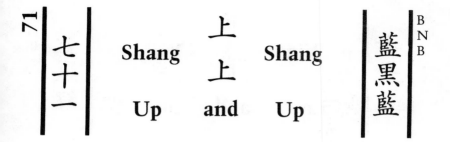

EXPLANATION: Between two Blues there is one Black. It means water giving rise to wood backward and forward. The image is an oceangoing ship sailing the seven seas fearless of winds and waves. This portends a great time to adventure forth.

JUDGMENT: Times are ripe and fortune is here. Seek wealth and receive wealth. Nothing will fail to flourish. Specially favorable for carrying trade abroad. Returning with a full load is assured.

COMMENTARY: This is a period of great vitality. You are enjoying the satisfaction of being strongly persuasive. With these attributes, one can, with a minimum of risk, entertain embarking on moderately speculative investments. But remember: no matter how many targets there are, the handling of ammunition is always dangerous.

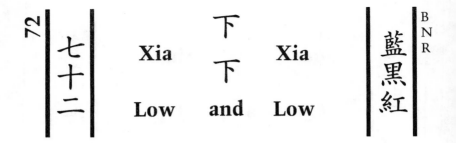

72 七十二 Xia 下下 Xia Low and Low 藍黑紅 B N R

EXPLANATION: Black follows Blue. Water cannot generate wood. But Black precedes Red. Water is just there to overcome fire. The image is an ice mountain that melts easily when the sun rises. The advice is against vanity and envy. The glitter of ice does not last long.

JUDGMENT: The fortunes are not favorable. Better remain humble and guard against loss. Wait out the time. If envy and vanity urge you ahead and you become opportunistic, there will be disaster and dishonor.

COMMENTARY: Do not let the motivation for becoming involved in an activity be because another appears to be enjoying great gain and influence by being involved in it. Especially beware of anyone who is anxious to sell you something because it is so profitable. Resist vanity and suppress envy. To endure humbly is to out-endure the glitter of ice.

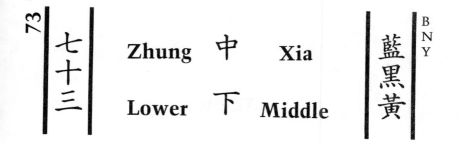

73 七十三 | Zhung 中 Xia | Lower 下 Middle | 藍黑黃 B N Y

EXPLANATION: When the cast gives an arrangement of Blue, Black, and Yellow, both relationships are reversed. Water does not generate wood and earth does not overcome water. The image is the traveler having a good change of heart, and the boat carrying him to the shore. Not good fortune, but danger is avoided with the grace of heaven.

JUDGMENT: Fortunes unfavorable. Do not risk venturing forth. Even though there is a possibility to correct the mistake, it will be a great scare. Better observe yourself, cultivate virtue, and wait for a better future.

COMMENTARY: Here is a situation in which there are many complications. As caution is the wiser side of courage, it is best not to become involved. However, should you have a change of mind and heart, it is possible that your native impulses may enable you to avoid disaster, but you will gain nothing at this time. Your best course is Wu Wei Wu (the action of nonaction).

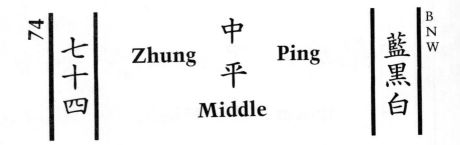

EXPLANATION: Casting Blue, Black, and White formulates another generating sequence in reverse. While the relationships of wood to water and water to metal are both friendly, no generation takes place. Therefore the image is to retire back to the woods and enjoy blissful leisure. The consultee should have the courage to retreat and abandon the ambitions of fortune and fame.

JUDGMENT: Prospects for fortune and wealth ordinary, but adequate to prevent cold and hunger. Do not envy others and invite trouble. Leave the business of others alone, thereby avoiding gossip.

COMMENTARY: Your present involvement is ill-advised. Rethink the facts and be sure that it was not envy that got you entangled. This is not clearly your business. Involvement only attracts trouble. The difficulties will compound as others begin to gossip. You may lose your honor and reputation unless you muster the courage to retire from the matter and abandon present hopes to attain fortune and fame.

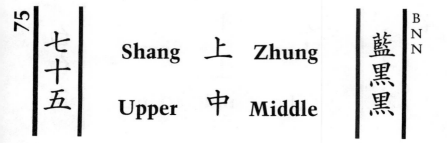

七十五

Shang 上 Zhung

Upper 中 Middle

藍黑黑

B
N
N

EXPLANATION: Two Blacks follow one Blue. While water does not generate wood, wood does receive the favorable support of flourishing water. The image is a bridge over the heavenly water, the magpie bridge formed over the Milky Way enabling the cowherd and the weaving maid to meet. The opportunity is good, and the heavens are calm.

JUDGMENT: A time of good fortune has arrived. The star of wealth shines. Unexpected opportunities are encountered. Good fortune comes from heaven. Congratulations.

COMMENTARY: The previous static conditions of frozen activity and barren existence have come to an end. A new season of spring begins, and new life with limitless potential begins to germinate. Amid all this fresh activity, you will discover unexpected opportunities and unanticipated support. Indulge in great study, develop understanding, and act compassionately.

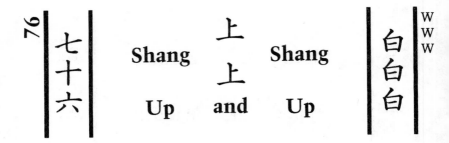

七十六 | Shang 上 Shang 上 Up and Up | 白 白 白 W W W

EXPLANATION: It is a forceful cast when three Whites turn up in a row. The energy of autumn and metal is at its height. The image is the full August moon. The fortunes of the consultee are full. No more worries. The clouds are cleared away and the whole earth is bright.

JUDGMENT: Fortune and wealth flourish in the extreme. The time is midautumn. The consultee should advance in the direction of *qian* (southwest). There he shall find his prize. Especially favorable for opening business. Portends great good fortune.

COMMENTARY: You are entering or in a period in which the efforts and investments of time and talent are coming to fruition. By lessening your intensity of drive and directing your attention to following things through to their conclusion, you will come upon great good fortune. This is the meaning of "advance in the direction of southwest." Areas of activity and interest which have long been in your mind are able to be launched and pursued by you at this time with strong prospects of being very successful.

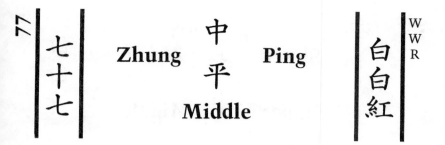

七十七　Zhung　中平　Ping　白白紅　WWR

Middle

EXPLANATION: To cast Red following two Whites indicates metal is not overcome by fire. The image is the great snow has just cleared, the red sun has risen. The difficult days have just passed, but a little wait is still necessary. When spring arrives, flourishing can be hoped for.

JUDGMENT: Wealth and fortune have passed the point of "splitting apart," and are about to "return." Good effects will manifest in the spring. Do not be impatient. There is hope for profit. But at this time, it is most necessary to proceed steadily forward in order to avoid unexpected expenditures.

COMMENTARY: Frozen assets (financial, intellectual, academic, physical, artistic, and spiritual), are about to thaw in an environment where the sun of harmonious conditions has risen. As the sun is just now rising, frozen things can reharden as unexpected clouds pass by. For this reason, you must persist steadily and unrelentingly to loosen and free that with which you desire to work and express yourself.

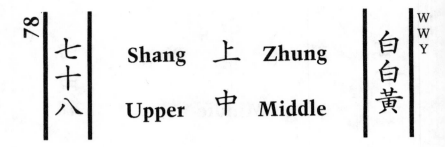

七十八 Shang 上 Zhung

Upper 中 Middle

白
白
黄

W
W Y

EXPLANATION: Yellow follows two Whites. Earth cannot generate metal from this position. But the power of metal is already doubled and strong. Thus the image is a treasured caldron emerging from the earth. The consultee will flourish with the time. His discoveries will be appreciated and great use made thereof.

JUDGMENT: Wealth and fortune are discovered at the proper time. Opportunities are right. Someone in a high position will support you and make good use of your services. The future promises both profit and fame.

COMMENTARY: From deep within your own creativity emerges an idea, dream, plan, or invention that will be the source of much good fortune for you. It may not necessarily be in terms of money, but in all events something very very satisfying and important to you is about to become possible. "Opportunities are right" does not mean that things are going to happen, but rather that you must be alert to opportunities and take hold upon them and utilize them for intended ends.

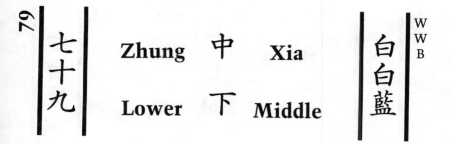

七十九 79 | Zhung 中 Xia | 白白藍 W W B

Lower 下 Middle

EXPLANATION: Two Whites precede one Blue. Wood is cut by metal to the extreme. But two metals together in the beginning still portends some wealth. The image indicates that a large beam is whittled down by incompetent carpenters. The consultee should guard his resources, but not be full of pride nor stingy. Employ people with care in order to prevent possible great loss.

JUDGMENT: Fortunes begin favorably. Wealth sought can be obtained. But after obtaining initial wealth, if you wish to develop the business, you must find competent and dependable help. To continue otherwise will certainly incur loses which will unfavorably affect both yourself and the family.

COMMENTARY: You have the possibility of being involved in a moderately thriving situation. But it requires the very strictest attention. The condition of that which can involve you is threatened by the incompetency of someone already associated with it. To terminate their involvement will create dissonance and encumber the smooth development of the project with unnecessary difficulties. Find a way to isolate and yet contain the vitiating element. This will ensure success.

133

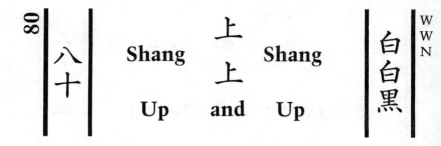

八十 80

Shang 上上 **Shang**

Up and **Up**

白白黑

W
W
N

EXPLANATION: To cast one Black following two Whites indicates the power of flourishing metal generating water. The image is springs and rivulets converging. The hundred streams are gathered. Great good fortune. Whatever kind of business is carried on is certain to prosper.

JUDGMENT: Wealth and fortune flow in continuously. Fame spreads abroad. Whatever the undertaking, flourishing success is certain.

COMMENTARY: The situation here is the coming together of many earlier contacts, suggestions, speculations, and previous relationships, with the resulting discovery that usable foundations have been established upon which new successes can be built. Some of these springs and rivulets may be underground. Do not hesitate to uncover them and use their power to generate success. How will you uncover them? Examine a map of the territory. Study thoroughly the location and anatomy of your present situation. You stand in the midst of affluence, do not keep it hidden!

134

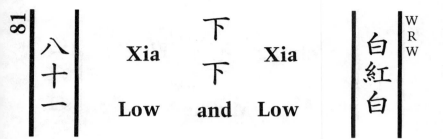

EXPLANATION: One Red sits between two Whites. Fire overcoming metal coming and going. Unfavorable for any progress. The image is nothing accomplished and the temples already having white hair. If one could have worked harder during youth and wasted less, there would not be the empty sighing at old age.

JUDGMENT: No hope for wealth. What is sought cannot be obtained. The only thing to do is to check old habits, practice frugality, continue working industriously; perhaps the hard times may relax a little.

COMMENTARY: You have been involved for a long time with certain things which have not been significantly fruitful. To wish that you had applied yourself more diligently and wasted less effort in frivolities will not fill the emptiness and loneliness of failure. Examine past destructive habits, act modestly, and be frugal, while continuing to work industriously as a novice in a new successful enterprise with fresh companions. This will bring a sense of dignity and meaningful reassurance to your life.

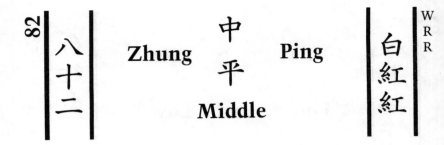

82 八十二 Zhung 中平 Ping Middle 白紅紅 W R R

EXPLANATION: The casting of one White preceding two Reds indicates metal is not overcome by fire. The image is bells (metal), protecting the blossoms of the garden. The consultee is in a favorable situation. There is help from someone of high position so that present prosperity may be maintained. But if one is dissatisfied and ambitious, the results will be less fortunate.

JUDGMENT: Fortune and wealth are ordinary. No great gain can be hoped for. But the situation is stable and the position secure. No need for concern.

COMMENTARY: At this time, you should not venture forth into any enterprise with excessively high hopes of great gains. The time is quite ordinary for you. Displaying an ability to plan and live within your present means will attract attention and admiration from an influential person interested in you. This will be the source of eventual help. Do not alienate the development of this friendship by voicing unhappy dissatisfaction with your present condition. To display and exercise ambitions which are not justifiable or supportable by your current circumstances is to cast doubt upon your reliability. Heed this advice so that the future will not be less fortunate.

136

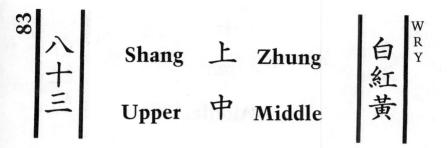

Shang 上 **Zhung**

Upper 中 **Middle**

白
红
黄

W
R
Y

EXPLANATION: White and Red are reversed. The overcoming of metal by fire is avoided. Yellow follows Red. Fire still generates earth. The image is to ride quickly to the southwest without looking back. Future is bright. Profit is to be gained from the southwest.

JUDGMENT: There is wealth and fortune. The prize can be gotten in the southwest. Great profit possible, but one must make haste.

COMMENTARY: The southwest indicates the "receptive" and "the gentle." The conditions for adventuring and experimenting are favorable. However, one should assay one's gear, resources, and strength before selecting an area to adventure into. The advice here seems to caution you to move in those areas where open-mindedness to innovation can be exercised and where you can arbitrate with gentleness the differences between fundamentalists and reformationists.

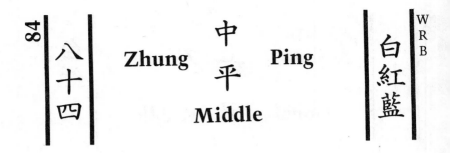

EXPLANATION: Red follows White. Fire does not overcome metal. Blue follows Red. Wood cannot generate fire. Neither generating nor overcoming. Neither honor nor disgrace. The image advises returning to the old family garden where the flowers are still red. Retreat more favorable than advance.

JUDGMENT: Fortune and wealth ordinary. Nothing exciting and no great deeds possible. Better return home and there still find enjoyment on the farm and in the garden.

COMMENTARY: It is a time of stillness. There is nothing in the present conditions that allows for any kind of activity. One is going through a phase of social and economic sterility. One is in a phenomenal limbo. The time is best utilized by turning the mind to retrospect on old ideas and old, never-acted-upon projects. When the energy vibrations about you change, then you will be ready for developing and growing new successes.

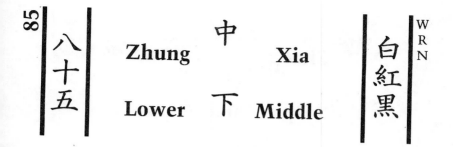

八十五 Zhung 中 Xia Lower 下 Middle 白 紅 黑 W R N

EXPLANATION: White, Red, and Black is the overcoming sequence in reverse. While fire does not overcome metal and water does not overcome fire, both relationships are hostile. This is not a lucky time. The image is a shepherd lost in the mountains. Forward there will be houses and people. Backward there are wild animals. If one knows the meaning of advance and retreat one will avoid bad fortune and find good fortune.

JUDGMENT: Times are unfavorable. Wealth is difficult to come by. Even exerting yourself, gains will only be slight. Still there may be chanced good luck if you concentrate on advancing. Loss of employment can be avoided. If you are timid and hesitating and back down, the situation will become disastrous.

COMMENTARY: Luck has been defined as "a force that brings good fortune or adversity." Hence, the phrase "this is not a lucky time" implies that this is a time when nothing is functioning influentially and nothing is capable of responding to influence. Because one is in still waters, one must row with great energy. There is neither tide nor current to assist you. But through self-initiated action, one will avoid worsening the situation.

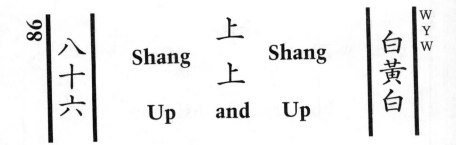

八十六 86

Shang 上上 Shang

Up and Up

白黄白 W Y W

EXPLANATION: Yellow in between two Whites. Earth generating metal backward and forward. The image is a man led into a treasure mountain. The consultee is about to reap a great profit. Good spirits are guiding one's way.

JUDGMENT: Fortune smooth and wealth certain. Profit in all directions. No matter what business is carried on, there will be rich returns. These come from favors of heaven and not merely from human endeavors.

COMMENTARY: What seems to be chance good luck is in fact the culmination of previous investments of time, money, understanding, and friendship with others that is manifesting in rich rewards. Your karma has attracted admirers. Many people are coming forth to support and encourage your endeavors. Congratulations.

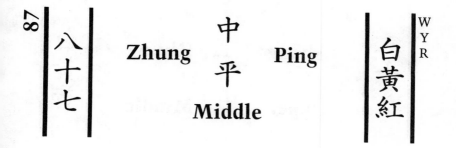

八十七 | **Zhung** 中平 **Ping** | 白黃紅 W Y R

Middle

EXPLANATION: White, Yellow, and Red flows against the stream. This is the generating sequence in reverse. Earth cannot generate metal and fire cannot generate earth. Therefore it is time to return to the farm and garden. The situation is not good, but the elements are friendly. Retreating, there is comfortable leisure at home.

JUDGMENT: While general destiny is good, fortunes are not flowing. If you contentedly pass your days, there will be no want or vexations. But if you wish to venture into business, you will need someone to help.

COMMENTARY: Things and conditions are more or less good. There is no threat of great disaster and no promise of excessive acquisition. By rowing rhythmically with the current, one will have smooth sailing. But should you wish to pluck a fruit from the trees on either shore, you will need the assistance of another.

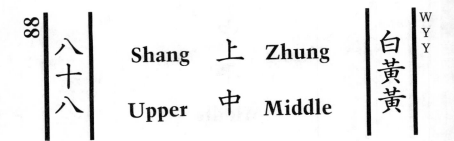

88 八十八 | Shang 上 Zhung

Upper 中 Middle | 白黄黄 W Y Y

EXPLANATION: Two Yellows follow one White. While earth cannot generate metal, the power of earth is flourishing, and thick foundations are established. This indicates that virtue has been accumulated and one may now rest secure in a favorable place. But the image points out also that this accumulation has started with bare hands. The difficulties already undergone are recognized.

JUDGMENT: Fortune and wealth will be long lasting. Much labor has been invested in the beginning. Now even the descendants will enjoy the fruit. But if you seek unrighteous gains, you will not obtain much.

COMMENTARY: The activities and dedication of the past have gained wide recognition among those persons and forces that are important to furthering your career. You have become the object of much admiration. Do not let the growing confidence of others in you seduce you into seeking unmerited privilege and gains from questionable means.

142

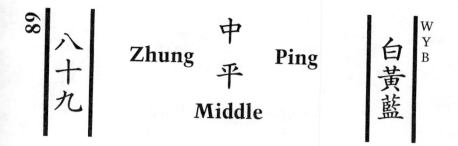

八十九　Zhung 中平 Ping　Middle　白黄藍　W Y B

EXPLANATION: Yellow follows White. Earth cannot generate metal. Blue follows Yellow. Wood does not overcome earth. Portends an even time. Nothing much will be accomplished. The image is the moon over the willow top. Quietly the gates remain closed. There may be some late fortune. Just enough to retire on.

JUDGMENT: Good times will come in your late years. The search for wealth is now in vain. To be cast adrift in the world without an understanding friend is unfortunate. But situations are peaceful and without vexations. This is a little good fortune.

COMMENTARY: The time is pleasant and uneventful. Opportunities are no longer opening up for you. What is to be gained must be gotten through your individual efforts and tenacity. You have lost contact with important old friends. It is permissible to entertain the nostalgia, but do not permit it to provoke you. To be able to enjoy the quietude of surcease is in itself good fortune.

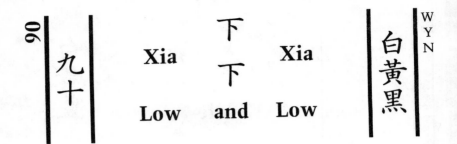

EXPLANATION: Yellow follows White. Earth cannot generate metal. Black follows Yellow. Water is overcome by earth. The image is the golden bell is broken and cast aside, but the pots and pans clash and jangle. Petty people are making waves and gossip rages. Good and evil are turned upside down.

JUDGMENT: Times are out of joint and fortune stagnates. It is not favorable for doing business. Losses are likely. Gossiping mouths are to be feared. At this time, one can only be content with heaven, close doors, and meditate at home. Then the waves will calm of themselves.

COMMENTARY: Affluence, influence, and authority have been sharply mollified. Envious competitors have conspired to campaign against you by inventing damaging gossip. No purpose is served at this time in trying to refute or to retaliate. Withdraw from the public arena and concentrate on reinforcing your virtue. In time the storm will of itself subside, having exhausted itself in the emptiness you provide for it.

144

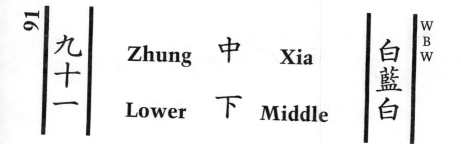

EXPLANATION: One Blue caught between two Whites. Wood is overcome by metal. The image is sickness added to poverty. Snow added to frost. Fortunately the second White follows the Blue, indicating a kindhearted person coming to assist and opening his pockets. One is saved from complete misfortune. Be grateful.

JUDGMENT: At the end of hope, something unexpected happens. Though the gain is not great, it is enough to take one out of immediate difficulties and thereby avoid impending cold and hunger.

COMMENTARY: You seem to be in the midst of annoying small difficulties. Misfortune piles upon misfortune. In addition to being confronted with obstacles, you find that you are being immobilized. Do not surrender all hope. From the depths of your intuitive awareness there will emerge an inspiring idea that unlocks hitherto unrealized talents. Aid will come to you from unexpected quarters.

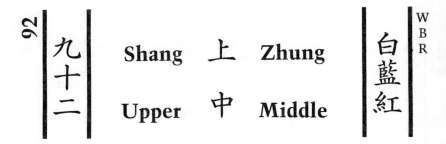

EXPLANATION: Blue follows White. Metal overcomes wood. Red follows Blue. Wood generates fire. The image is the sun appearing after clouds and rain. Taking a walk, blossoms smile in one's path. There is about to be a breakthrough after some dark days.

JUDGMENT: Fortune and wealth have turned from "stagnation" to "peace." Happy events are ahead. If you are opening some business, society will welcome it. Triple profit can be expected.

COMMENTARY: You have been in a period of disappointment and low spirit. Now things are about to change. As you become involved in social and economic projects, you will attract opportunities of service that will be most rewarding. The substance of your fortune will be determined by the care you exercise in selecting a field of endeavor.

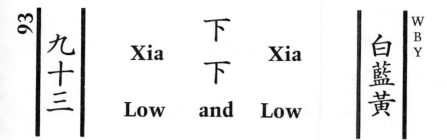

九十三

Xia 下下 Xia

Low and Low

白藍黃 W B Y

EXPLANATION: With this cast, White precedes Blue. Metal cuts wood. Blue precedes Yellow. Wood cracks earth. Overcoming is repeated. The image is the roof beam unable to bear great weight. The house is about to fall into rubble. The meaning is clear. Disaster and failure for business and family.

JUDGMENT: A destructive star presides. Disasters repeat. Nothing is favorable. How can you seek wealth? Better that you cultivate your virtues. Only then will there be a chance for fortunes to improve in the future.

COMMENTARY: What can be seen by the light of "a destructive star" is a misshapen shape. What appears to have one shape upon closer scrutiny is revealed to have another. Hence any decisions or plans made under these conditions are contaminated with the possibilities of error and inherent dangers. When one cannot clearly see the target, it is better not to aim. Since change is the inescapable constant, one can find security in waiting to escape through the inescapable.

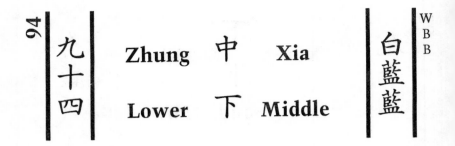

Zhung 中 **Xia**

Lower 下 **Middle**

EXPLANATION: Blue following White is metal overcoming wood. But Blue is repeated, which indicates that the energies of wood are still strong. Although one must now endure hardships and cold, the vegetation will flourish again when spring returns.

JUDGMENT: The flow of fortune and wealth are blocked for the present. The fall and winter will be especially difficult. One must be careful to prevent loss. Only after much hardship will there be a return of fortune.

COMMENTARY: The present is like a deciduous tree in winter that is barren, having no leaves or fruit. But hidden beneath its skeletal nakedness, the energies of renewal lie dormant, awaiting the spring. At this time you must be frugal. By watering and fertilizing in the middle of winter one will not succeed in forcing growth upon a spring and summer plant. Growth will begin in the proper season. A wise man waits for signs from nature.

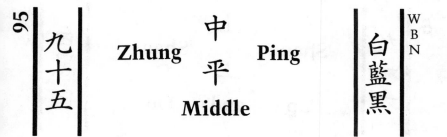

EXPLANATION: Blue follows White. Metal overcomes wood. Black follows Blue. Water cannot generate wood, but may still be supportive. Therefore the damage to wood from metal may still be healed.

JUDGMENT: This is not the time for fortune and wealth. Attempts to advance will be in vain. Do not contend with the world but retire to the woods and stream. If you carry on business, there may be some empty fame, but no real profit.

COMMENTARY: The hard fact of the present situation is that it is untenable. It is like being aboard a sailing vessel on a calm sea where there is not a single breeze to drive the sails. No purpose in hoisting the sails. Pull out the old rod and fish from the rail. The catch, while not of much profit, may bring you some little fame. To fish from the rail means to entice from your depths new ideas.

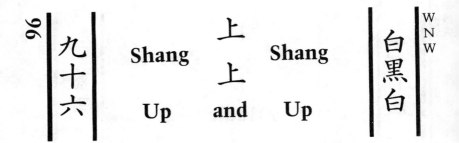

九十六

Shang 上上 Shang

Up and Up

白黑白

W N W

EXPLANATION: One Black between two Whites. Metal generates water backwards and forward. The image is the fisherman dropping his line and making a big catch after only a little wait. Good fortunes are here. Occasion for rejoicing.

JUDGMENT: Fortune and wealth flow. What is sought will be obtained. Only a small wait and the prize is yours. Great profit without much labor. In speculative ventures, others will assist with finances.

COMMENTARY: This is a period of exceptional opportunity for you. You are in the right spot at the right time, your slightest effort will be rewarded. While you will not have much difficulty in getting backers to finance your ambitions, you must be extraordinarily perspicacious in selecting a project to promote.

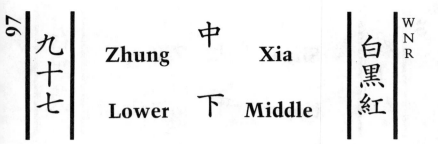

九十七　　Zhung 中 Xia

Lower 下 Middle

白
黒
紅

W
N
R

EXPLANATION: Black follows White. Metal generates water. Red follows Black. Water overcomes fire. First generating then overcoming produces the image of first flourishing then declining. Thus one is advised against overindulging in enjoyments and becoming proud with riches. Failure and decline is immanent. Be careful.

JUDGMENT: Wealth and fortune turn from "peace" to "stagnation." Fullness invites diminution. But if you will heed the warning to avoid self-indulgence and pride, you may remain full by giving to others.

COMMENTARY: All things experience the cyclicity of coming and going. So with fame, wealth, and fortune, there is a time of expansion and a time of diminishing. As one's affluence lessens, one can hold on to honor and respect by being modest in deportment, compassionate in relationships, and cheerful in giving to others. When conditions change there will be many to help you up again.

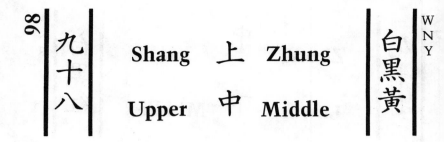

九十八

Shang 上 Zhung

Upper 中 Middle

白黒黃

W
N
Y

EXPLANATION: Black follows White. Metal generates water. Yellow follows Black. Earth does not overcome water. Thus the image is fresh water clearing away dust and obstacles. Fate flourishes mid-course. Business and family fortunes are renewed.

JUDGMENT: Wealth and fortune flourish. Foundations are reestablished. Future obstacles are cleared away. Destiny is strong beyond the ordinary.

COMMENTARY: This is an auspicious time for you. Take advantage of the energy vibrations to reactivate old projects and initiate new ones. The determining causes by which things come to be are fully supportive of your every desire and intention. Think ethically and act compassionately, and great success will crown your days.

152

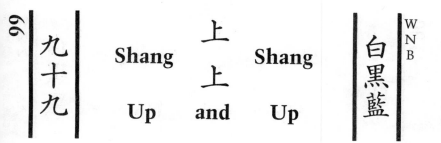

EXPLANATION: White, Black, and Blue are in the generating sequence all the way through. Metal generates water, and water generates wood. The image is a pleasure boat sailing in a clear lake lined with flowers to show the happiness of the fortunes.

JUDGMENT: Wealth and fortune all smooth. Everything is satisfying. Free and unencumbered, great joy is in store for you.

COMMENTARY: This is a time of happiness and pleasure. To encumber a joyous spirit with the burden of mundane concerns is like putting a black lens on a flashlight: one cannot use its rays to reveal things. This is a time for keeping the heart light and the mind bouncing. Do not permit either to rest heavily upon a single moment. When fruits are ripe, they should be eaten. There is no purpose or need to fertilize them.

153

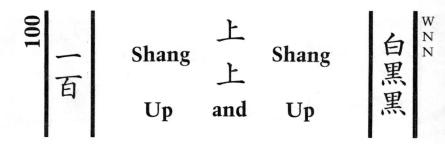

EXPLANATION: Two Blacks follow one White. Metal generates flourishing water. The fortunes of "peace" open from heaven, flowing forth without end. If the consultee goes into business, great flourishing is certain.

JUDGMENT: Times are right. Great springs of fortune open. No matter what kind of business, all will be smooth, and great profit flows.

COMMENTARY: Tremendous energy is flowing. Now is the time to tune in and channel the cosmic forces into service. Good fortune in abundance will attend the person who goes into a business that is unique and noncompetitive. It should be a business that offers a service or product that is so individual that there is no other like it. In this way it will be noncompetitive and so harmonize with the fortunes of "peace," which flow from heaven without end.

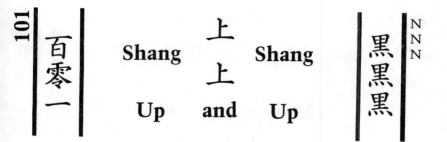

EXPLANATION: Three Blacks together is a strong casting. The power of water at its height. Response will come from the north in the *k'an* position. The image is sailing the ocean with the six great tortoises in harness. The consultee is sure to reap great profit.

JUDGMENT: Wealth and fortune come in the winter season. Best search in the north. The prize can be gained. Keep the spirits high. Great riches soon.

COMMENTARY: Chinese compass arrangements situate north at the bottom. The *kua* (trigram) is called *k'an*. Its position symbolizes going down deeply into, and so it is called "the abysmal." We often translate it as "fathomable mystery." You are presently in a masterful position "sailing the ocean with the six great tortoises in harness." Success is all about you. You have only to delve into the mystery of your intuitive self to fathom a direction and focus for applying your abilities with exceptional success.

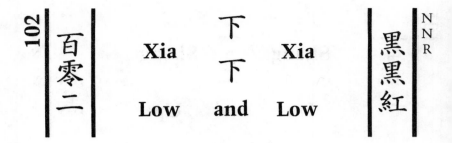

百零二　　Xia　下下　Xia　黑黑紅　N N R

Low　and　Low

EXPLANATION: One Red follows two Blacks. Fire overcome by water to the extreme. The image is walking over a dangerous bridge by night and the lamp is blown out. The consultee is confronting times of great peril. Nothing should be undertaken. With great caution, destruction may perhaps be avoided.

JUDGMENT: Time of great danger. Even though someone has tried to guide you, you have failed to listen. Tremble and beware.

COMMENTARY: You are in a period of confusion and going through a phase in which it is difficult for you to see things clearly. Even though some offer to help you, because of an inner cloudiness to your perception, in reaching for their hand, you miss it and so lose your footing. Become quiet and wait until a light pierces the darkness and you can see and understand more clearly.

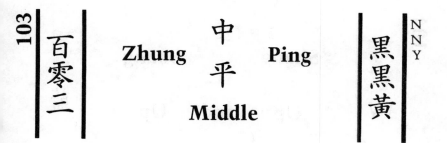

Zhung 中平 Ping

Middle

EXPLANATION: Two Blacks precede one Yellow. One earth cannot overcome two waters. But the overflowing waters are redirected by the wise use of a little earth. Therefore the image is that of the Great Yu controlling the floods. If the consultee is in business some profit can be gained only after great hardship.

JUDGMENT: Fortunes ordinary. Nothing special can be gained. With steady management and long patience, there can be small profit.

COMMENTARY: As one views the situation, one sees that which is desired escaping past one and going off in a different direction. With the exercise of a little ingenuity, it is possible to attract and redirect the profit-getting energies so that you too can be nourished.

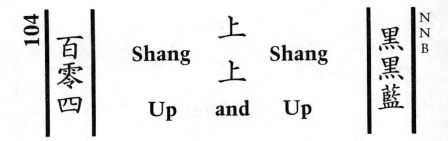

EXPLANATION: One Blue follows two Blacks. Wood is generated by flourishing water. The consultee is at a time when great deeds may be accomplished. Not only will there be both fame and fortune, but the accomplishments will endure long.

JUDGMENT: Great wealth and fortune. Long-lasting future. Extraordinary accomplishments in business. Firm foundations can be established to support many generations. Honor and fame also in store.

COMMENTARY: You are enveloped by intensely strong positive energies. Any idea carefully planned, wisely located, and efficiently instrumented is destined to enjoy development, popularity, and great success. The time is ideal for setting firm foundations and establishing an enviable reputation.

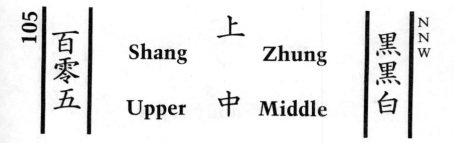

105

百零五

Shang 上 Zhung

Upper 中 Middle

黑黑白

N
N W
W

EXPLANATION: One White follows two Blacks. Metal cannot generage water, but their relationship is friendly. The image is a pearl recovered washed onto shore. The kind in heart will be rewarded by heaven. Abide with one's innate good nature, and both business and family will prosper again.

JUDGMENT: Fortune has turned. What is sought will be obtained. What is lost will be recovered. Unexpected wealth may be found. The protection of heaven changes dangers into safety.

COMMENTARY: Frozen assets cannot be used. But their confirmed existence can facilitate the acquiring of resources which enable ongoing activity and expansion. An investment, either in business or in a human relationship, long forgotten or thought to be lost, will reemerge to your joy and profit.

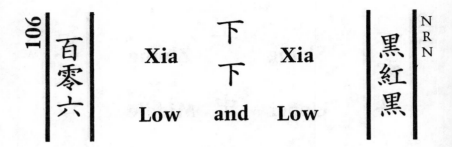

EXPLANATION: One Red is held between two Blacks. Fire is overcome by water coming and going. The conflict of the elements conveys the image of yin and yang out of harmony. The consultee should reflect carefully upon his situation.

JUDGMENT: Times are out of whack. Wealth is without hope. Be content with your lot and cultivate yourself. Clear your mind and simplify your desires; otherwise you will remain trapped as in an "abyss," ☵ , one long yang surrounded by yins.

COMMENTARY: While you may be enjoying a sufficiency of material things—money, position, status, and so on—you experience marked dissatisfaction. The dark overcast is within. You are like one who has pulled down a black shade over the window and declared "the day is gone." You have many means for acquiring happiness at your disposal. To use them, clear your mind through honest introspection and simplify your desires.

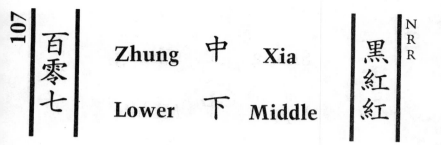

百零七　Zhung　中　Xia

Lower　下　Middle

N
R R
R

黑
紅
紅

EXPLANATION: Two Reds follow one Black. Much fire is injured by water. The image is waves of flower petals felled by the storm. Fortunes are declining. No one pities. Better shut the doors to reflect upon one's past mistakes and wait for a better time.

JUDGMENT: Fortunes are "splitting apart." There is danger of losing wealth. Whoever is engaged in business or investment better close and withdraw before greater loss is incurred. To be brave and retreat is the wise course.

COMMENTARY: The security and confidence enjoyed up until now is being shaken. The indications of the time are not advantageous. It is almost as if a time of panic were beginning to brew. Struggle will become commonplace. Heed the advice to withdraw. Retreat to a quiet space and reexamine your successes and failures of the past. Store up the results of these analyses for using when better times return.

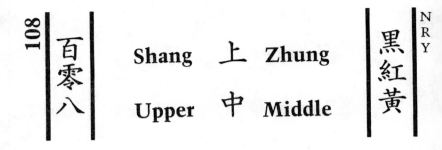

EXPLANATION: Red follows Black. Water overcomes fire. Yellow follows Red. Fire generates earth. What is stored in the winter sprouts again in the spring. The image is the old being removed and the new emerging. Times have turned.

JUDGMENT: Fortunes and wealth are first stagnant, then smooth. The time of flourishing begins after winter solstice and peaks in the spring. It is not long to wait. Do not be impatient.

COMMENTARY: Conditions are flaccid, and the time is not yet come when things will develop quickly. Take care of and protect that which is hibernating. When the wintertime of prospecting is complete, hidden energies will begin to stir and new developments manifest. The time is so close that one must not allow anxiety or impatience to provoke premature action.

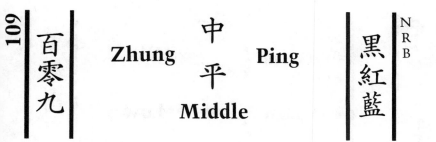

EXPLANATION: Red follows Black. Water overcomes fire. Blue follows Red. Wood cannot generate fire. The image is the rain dousing the fire, but the sky clears and more wood can be gathered. While wood is not in a position to generate fire at present, the relationship is supportive. After much hardship, there appears a chance for recovery.

JUDGMENT: The search for wealth will be very difficult in the beginning. Then some gain may be possible. But it will be only sufficient to keep off wants. If you can be content in poverty, the way out remains open, and life energies continue to flow.

COMMENTARY: It is an edgy time, and one feels the weight of many pressures that tend to be discouraging. It is most important at this time to maintain your own courage and present a countenance of confidence. Soon the pressures will subside, and conditions will change enabling an active program of fresh productivity.

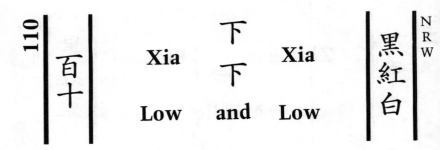

EXPLANATION: Black, Red, and White form a continuous sequence of overcoming. Water overcomes fire, and fire overcomes metal. The image is a sick man evading the doctor. One mistake added to another. If the consultee will begin to understand his situation and work on reforming himself, perhaps he may recover. Otherwise all will be without hope.

JUDGMENT: Fortunes are malevolent. Calamities repeated. Life energies nearly exhausted. But even in this situation, if you will arouse yourself and change your ways, survival is possible. Do not just sit and blame fate or others. That only brings the end faster.

COMMENTARY: You are caught in one of those periods when it seems that you are wrong if you do and wrong if you don't. Perhaps it is not that everyone is dissatisfied with you, but rather with your ways of being you. You may resolve a great deal if you will retire into yourself and examine everything you find, then test it. This will help you to change some of your ways, and like a rower who learns to draw the oar through the water correctly, his ship sails more easily and more quickly.

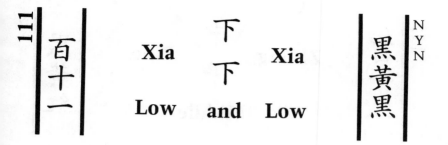

EXPLANATION: One Yellow between two Blacks. Earth overcomes water. But now water, front and back, floods over the earth. The image is waves driven by wind attacking the dikes repeatedly. The consultee must use care and exercise endurance, otherwise troubles will multiply and vexations continue.

JUDGMENT: Fortunes are bad. Troubles ahead. Gossip and accusations are coming endlessly. The only thing to do is to step carefully and try to endure the disadvantages. Do not be willful and become involved in more disputes. Otherwise greater losses are certain.

COMMENTARY: This seems to portend the approach of legal difficulties, hassles involving complicated points and counter-points. There is great verbosity and thundering oratory. Hold your temper and still your tongue. Only by enduring patiently with humility will you be able to gain a position from which you can act with strength. Practice the art of letting your opponent's aggression defeat him, for in the very exercising of it, he will eventually exhaust himself.

百十二 Zhung 中平 Ping 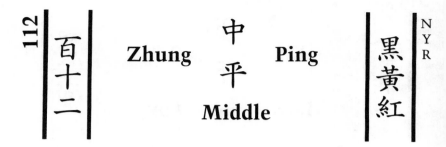 黑黄紅 N Y R

Middle

EXPLANATION: Yellow follows Black. Earth cannot overcome water. Red follows Yellow. Fire cannot generate earth. Nothing much happens. A good time to pause and reflect upon the laws of fortune. Become familiar with the principles of generating and overcoming.

JUDGMENT: Wealth and fortune ordinary. Nothing outstanding is about to happen. If you will reflect upon the principles of advancing and retreating, the awareness will certainly help you ahead in another day.

COMMENTARY: There is little that is impressive about this period for you. There is nothing truly exciting to engage your interest, nor can you find a sufficiently meaningful response to any efforts you may initiate. In times such as these, it is best to refrain from acts of assertiveness, to prepare for a time more conducive to successful activity; ponder upon the laws of energy and study the principles of interaction and exchange.

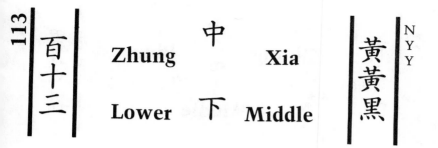

Zhung 中 Xia

Lower 下 Middle

N
Y
Y

EXPLANATION: Two Yellows follow one Black. Earth does not overcome water. But with earth doubled, water is covered. The image is digging a well and not yet reaching the water. If the consultee is trying to conduct business, much effort will be wasted. Better meditate upon your innate good nature and piously pray to the waters as the ancients were wont to do.

JUDGMENT: Fortunes are obstructed. Search for wealth will be disappointing. Much calculated effort remains in vain. Cultivate your virtues and the spring may open of itself.

COMMENTARY: Your involvement at this time is extracting a great deal of energy from you. Thought, time, and labor are being dissipated upon inconsequential trivia. Pause and give some thought to your own good nature and seek a way to attune harmoniously with the situation at hand. In time, with the arrival of spring (proper conditions), things will begin to move of themselves and you will begin to progress.

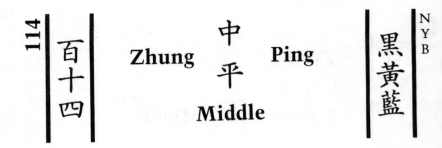

114 百十四 **Zhung** 中平 **Ping** 黑黄藍 N Y B

Middle

EXPLANATION: In this casting, Black, Yellow, and Blue are in the overcoming sequence, but the order is fortunately reversed. Thus earth does not check water and wood does not break earth. The image simply indicates a hazardous path and warns against retreat or a lapse of effort. Advance is favorable.

JUDGMENT: Wealth and fortune are not smooth, but if you press ahead diligently, gains are to be gotten. If you shrink from hardship and stay home, there will be no opportunity. Retreat is worse.

COMMENTARY: The situation is common and usual. There are no advantages or disadvantages attending it. To be successful requires clear thinking, hard work, and diligent persistence. In this way, the usual hazards that attend these matters can be avoided, and one will not have to retreat. Retreat brings disaster.

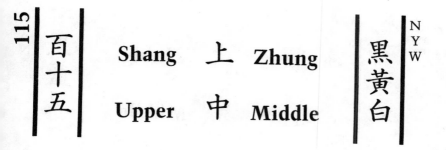

百十五 Shang 上 Zhung

Upper 中 Middle

黑黄白

N Y W

EXPLANATION: Yellow follows Black. Earth does not overcome water. White follows Yellow. Earth generates metal. The image is sweet spring and fertile earth covered by light snow. The consultee has come upon a flourishing time. Great profit is promised.

JUDGMENT: Great hope for flourishing wealth and fortune. Present situation peaceful and secure. What is established will prosper. Great profit to follow. Favorable to advance.

COMMENTARY: You are presently in the midst of good vibrations and creative energy. The gods and imps are pleased with your intentions and the integrity of your efforts. Keep to your values, pursue virtue, and be compassionate. In this way you will hold the enduring protection of heaven.

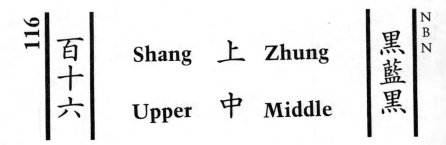

EXPLANATION: The cast returns one Blue between two Blacks. Water generates wood backward and forward. The image is the harnessing of two dragons. Both fame and fortune are in store.

JUDGMENT: Great power of wealth and fortune. Favorable to start large undertaking and take control. There will be high fame and great profit.

COMMENTARY: Great affluence is within your reach. Time and talent have matured together. Your previous experiences interrelate in such a way that they have become positive supplements to each other, resulting in a dynamic ability to achieve whatever goals you select.

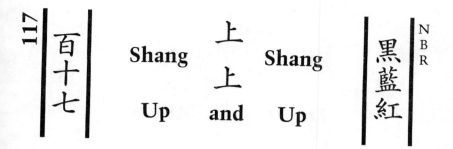

EXPLANATION: Black, Blue, and Red is casting a generating sequence. Water generates wood, and wood generates fire. The image is picking herbs in the mountain. One follows the path of water and trees and mounts up to heaven. If the consultee is interested in the undertaking, he is sure to enter a blissful realm.

JUDGMENT: Fortunes are excellent. All will be smooth. Whatever is sought will be gained. Each step will lead to one higher. There are also hidden opportunities and someone will help from the background. Whether for fame or fortune, achievement is sure.

COMMENTARY: "Picking herbs in the mountain" is to carefully select the small things which will add a spice to life. To "follow the path of water and trees" means to be alert to obstacles and prepared to circumvent them, to be on the lookout for practical aspects, such as traditions, techniques, and so on, which afford one something solid and tangible for attaching one's energies to. Good fortune is seeking you; do not run ahead of it too quickly.

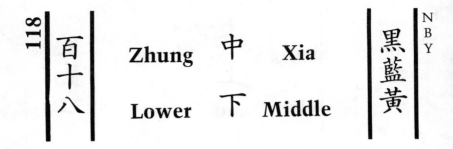

Zhung 中 Xia

Lower 下 Middle

EXPLANATION: This casting begins with Blue following Black. Water generating wood. But Yellow following Blue is wood overcoming earth. The image is a boat that starts out sailing with the wind. But the wind changes, and one is forced to the shore. The meaning is very clear.

JUDGMENT: Wealth and fortune first smooth then obstructed. But opposition can be met with acceptance. Stopping progress one can hold secure. There will be no great harm. If we risk the danger and proceed, there may well be the disaster of capsizing. Beware.

COMMENTARY: Conditions are presently very comfortable. But it is best that you keep an eye out for the weather. Sudden winds can bring unexpected clouds heavy with storming rains. It may be that a temporary shutdown will help you to maintain a hold upon your course. In a word, watch out and be ready to drop an anchor at a moment's notice. It may delay your reaching a fortune, but to dare the fates will surely be ruinous.

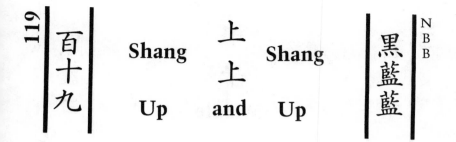

Shang 上上 **Shang**

Up and Up

黑藍藍

EXPLANATION: Two Blues follow one Black. Water generates wood, and wood flourishes luxuriantly. The image is a blue bridge formed over the silver river. Good fortune is here, a path is opened to the clouds.

JUDGMENT: The path to great wealth and fortune is open. Some extraordinary happy meeting is destined beyond expectations. Great happiness is in store. If the consultee is concerned with marriage, the prospects are especially satisfying.

COMMENTARY: Certain things will seem like a fairy tale, and there is a sense of euphoria that accompanies your involvement with them. The time abounds with good fortune that is coming your way. Remain true to your own virtues. Avoid the immorality found in high places and have a gentle word for the anguished.

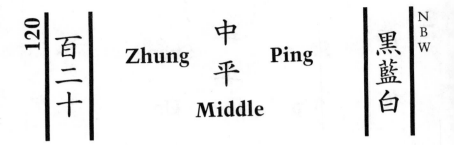

EXPLANATION: Here Blue follows Black. Water generates wood. White follows Blue. Metal does not overcome wood. The image is the willow branch sprinkling sweet dew, and the dry wood sprouts again as in spring. If the consultee will hold to his innate good nature, he will be blessed by heaven.

JUDGMENT: Fortune has turned. Wealth can be obtained. Because of your kind nature, you have elicited help from powerful ones. Like a grounded fish saved by the returning tide, recovery is at hand.

COMMENTARY: The situation has been tense. The prospect of loss has been imminent. Uncalculated good deeds are like forgotten reserves, they emerge with redeeming effectiveness, often when most needed. Here you are about to get help because of past considerations to others. Anxiety is real, but do not despair.

174

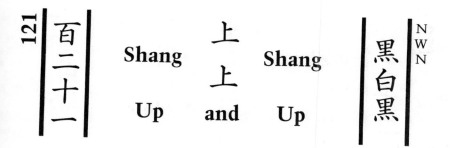

Shang 上上 **Shang**

Up and **Up**

EXPLANATION: One White between two Blacks. Water is generated by metal backward and forward. The image is a hole opened for a pond, and springs of water flow in from left and right. Wealth is sure to prosper. All affairs will proceed smoothly.

JUDGMENT: The source of wealth is wide open. Opportunities are found everywhere. The northwest promises especially great profits. Whatever is undertaken will succeed.

COMMENTARY: The indications suggested here are that you have resources at hand which can be used in acquiring greater affluence. The promises indicated as being in the northwest refers to there being many excellent opportunities waiting in businesses and other projects which are either long established and are being offered for new proprietorship, or which appear to be in decline and are available for fresh and innovative management.

175

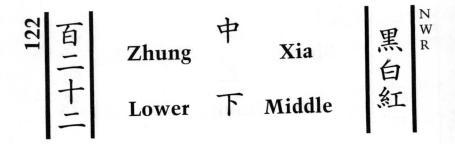

百
二
十
二

Zhung 中 Xia

Lower 下 Middle

黑
白
紅

N
W
R

EXPLANATION: Metal cannot generate water. Red follows White. While metal is not overcome by fire, their relationship is not harmonious. The image is someone struggling under another's roof and making marriage garments for another. Fortunes do not flourish. Hard work only yields subsistence.

JUDGMENT: After half a life's labor, the fortunes are still ordinary. Working for others. Though the profits can be great, your share is slight. Nothing more can be hoped for. This is your fate. No use complaining.

COMMENTARY: This casting has two distinct meanings. The one intended for the consultee is determined more or less by his age. If he is advanced in years, the cast is a simple statement of fact. If after a lifetime you are still working for others, "nothing more can be hoped for." If cast by a younger person, this is a warning to get out of a rut and begin to make wedding garments to your own measurement instead of always for another. One should begin working industriously for others in one's youth but only with the idea of being able to avoid the full costs of one's mistakes. When experience has taken in most of the mistakes, it's time to move out on your own and wisely be capable of paying for another youth's mistakes.

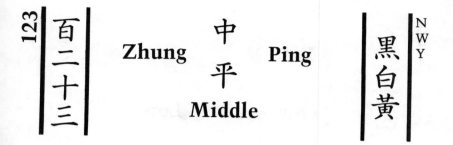

百
二
十
三

Zhung 中 **Ping**
平
Middle

黑
白
黃

EXPLANATION: Black, White, and Yellow is the generating sequence, but here they are reversed. Thus metal cannot generate water, and earth cannot generate metal. The image is the watery reflection of palaces and pavillions. Reversed and illusory. The consultee may gain some empty fame but no real profit.

JUDGMENT: Wealth and fortune not very smooth. Though something may be gained, it soon fades away. Hard on the outside but dry inside, displaying an empty shell.

COMMENTARY: The situation here calls for great depth of perception and confirmed information that enables you to make decisions and act with certitude. Many prospects offered will be in actuality the reverse of what they seem to be. Test them for substance, then test them for quality of material they are made of. Caution is needed in considering any new offers and in directing old and familiar projects.

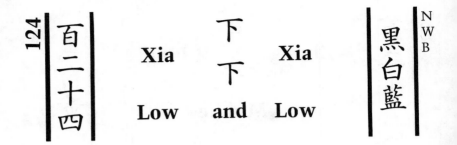

EXPLANATION: Black and White turned around. Metal cannot generate water. But White precedes Blue. Wood is overcome by metal. The image is changeable friends like the shapes of clouds. World situations and human relationships are all changeable. The consultee must be careful so as not to fall prey to the schemes of petty people.

JUDGMENT: Fortunes are not good. You have not encountered any good honest people. Avoid making friends indiscriminately. When you join in business with others, you are likely to be had. Be careful.

COMMENTARY: You are walking down the midway at a country fair. All about you are tricksters and illusionists. Everything is facade. The barker who looks down at you saying "my good friend" is merely using the language of social grace to accomplish a rascally end. Do not let everyone that says "friend" enter into the affections of your heart.

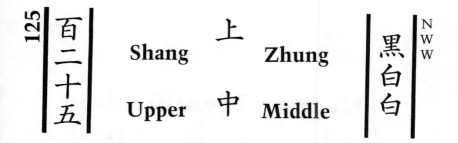

EXPLANATION: Two Whites follow one Black. While water cannot be generated from metal in this order, the power of metal (that is, of gold) is great. The image is "the game of Go is over. The Whites win. The prize is gold. The fates are determined."

JUDGMENT: Wealth and fortune flourish. The prospect of winning the prize is immediate. The search should proceed due west. Any business conducted will win over competitions, and triple profit can be expected.

COMMENTARY: This is a very fortuitous casting. But it may be misunderstood. While it seems to indicate that everything is a fully realized and accomplished fact, it has an important instruction hidden in it. "The fates are determined" means that while you have everything you need for great success, it still requires strong determination exercised through hard work and persistence against any odds that arise. "The prospect of winning" is another hint that things are not falling in your lap while you sleep, but that waking energy must be exerted with what is immediately about you. "The search should proceed due west" means that you should pursue your goal to the end. There you will find great, unexpected, and flourishing success.

Casting Identification Chart for Upper Red

SIGN NUMBER	UPPER	MIDDLE	LOWER	LEGEND
1	R	R	R	Triple light. Projection of cosmic energy.
2	R	R	Y	Earth born out of fire. Yang ascending.
3	R	R	B	Fire precedes wood, growth can flourish.
4	R	R	W	Double fire attacks stubborn metal. Self-check.
5	R	R	N	Double fire threatens water. Retreat reverses.
6	R	Y	R	Earth between two fires. Broadly efficacious.
7	R	Y	Y	Earthly slope receiving energy. Harmonize with times.
8	R	Y	B	Earth after fire supports new growth. Inner strength.
9	R	Y	W	Earth after fire exposing metal. Regenerative energies.
10	R	Y	N	Earth after fire flooded by water. Separate illusion from fact.
11	R	B	R	Stream between fruitful banks. Seeker open to guidance.

SIGN	NUMBER	UPPER	MIDDLE	LOWER	LEGEND
	12	R	B	Y	Wood cannot start fire. Avoid disaster, retreat.
	13	R	B	B	Trees' shade give protection from sun. Develop self-sufficiency.
	14	R	B	W	Water extinguishes fire. No external help. Tread water.
	15	R	B	N	Wood, fire, and water all in nonproductive order. Retire.
	16	R	W	R	Fire reveals metal melted by fire. Effort is vain.
	17	R	W	Y	Fire releases metal, metal lost in earth. Analyse and replan.
	18	R	W	B	Fire releases metal which resists wood. Express no discontent.
	19	R	W	W	Fire refines metal. Great hardships lead to rewards.
	20	R	W	N	Fire releases metal generating water. Struggle is rewarded.
	21	R	N	R	Water overcomes fire, yet fire persists. Seek to avoid.
	22	R	N	Y	From earth comes water for use with fire. Act but do not oppose.
	23	R	N	B	Vegetation is nourished. Progress after midpoint.
	24	R	N	W	Flowers on water shade fishes. Uneventful time.
	25	R	N	N	Sun is hidden behind rain clouds. A good change in fortune.

Casting Identification Chart for Upper Yellow

SIGN NUMBER	UPPER	MIDDLE	LOWER	LEGEND
26	Y	Y	Y	Power of earth is great. Regard ancestors.
27	Y	Y	R	Earth upon earth hides fire. Hidden reserves.
28	Y	Y	B	Much earth bears trees. Cultivate industriousness.
29	Y	Y	W	Earthly powers produce gold. Attend to virtue.
30	Y	Y	N	Looming earth with narrow obstructions. Great caution.
31	Y	R	Y	Fire centered in earth. Treasures revealed.
32	Y	R	R	Earth supporting much fire. Great supportive harmony.
33	Y	R	B	Nonproductive time. Be inactive and retrospective.
34	Y	R	W	No generating, no overcoming. Must wait for better future.
35	Y	R	N	Situation dormant. Sustain through simple industry.

SIGN NUMBER	UPPER	MIDDLE	LOWER	LEGEND
36	Y	B	Y	Wood buried in earth. No recognition of talent.
37	Y	B	R	Luxuriant woods in mountain. Seeker harmonizes.
38	Y	B	B	Earth sustaining wood. Eastward lies fortune.
39	Y	B	W	Metal negates wood which overcomes earth. Avoid nostalgia.
40	Y	B	N	Situation affords no benefits. Joys are illusory.
41	Y	W	Y	Earth producing metal. Gold in earth, profits ahead.
42	Y	W	R	Earth yields metal resisting fire. Wealth properly attained.
43	Y	W	B	Metal exuding from earth may be crated in wood.
44	Y	W	W	Double power of gold. Success now attainable.
45	Y	W	N	Earth produces metal generating water. Receptivity.
46	Y	N	Y	Water locked within earth. Stalemate. Meditate.
47	Y	N	R	Difficult mountain, nonfordable stream. Patience.
48	Y	N	B	Earth overcomes water growing things. Belated fortune.
49	Y	N	W	Water overcomes earth. Disharmony. Return to principles.
50	Y	N	N	Waters in floodtide. Important to observe teaching.

Casting Identification Chart for Upper Blue

SIGN	NUMBER	UPPER	MIDDLE	LOWER	LEGEND
	51	B	B	B	Triple strength wood. Help comes from many sources.
	52	B	B	R	Wood generating fire. Time is efficacious for ideas.
	53	B	B	Y	Much wood covers earth. Many pressures hinder action.
	54	B	B	W	Too much wood, little metal. Insufficient strength.
	55	B	B	N	In the woods a river. Needed support available.
	56	B	R	B	Wood produces great fire. Pursue family and business.
	57	B	R	R	Wood generates double fire. Conditions right for every effort.
	58	B	R	Y	Fruits ripening in heaven. Polish up ideas. Opportunity.

184

SIGN	NUMBER	UPPER	MIDDLE	LOWER	LEGEND
	59	B	R	W	Wood to fire melting metal. Surrounded by envy and gossip. Retire.
	60	B	R	N	Wood makes fire unharmed by water. Hope for profit.
	61	B	Y	B	Earth overcome by wood. Beset with problems. Retreat.
	62	B	Y	R	Wood covers earth. Ability is hidden, talents left unused.
	63	B	Y	Y	Wood shades great acres. Earth enriched. Sincerity brings fortune.
	64	B	Y	W	Wood covers earth giving metal. There is vacillation. Advance.
	65	B	Y	N	Wood covers earth hiding water. Retreat. Avoid despair.
	66	B	W	B	Metal destroys wood in both directions. Impasse. Wait.
	67	B	W	R	Fire yields to metal yielding to wood. Unfriendly, precarious time.
	68	B	W	Y	No overcoming, no generating. Time not suited for adventure.
	69	B	W	W	Rock is found in thorn bush. Hostility followed by rewards.
	70	B	W	N	A small boat sailing many lakes. Opportunity for business nears.
	71	B	N	B	Water gives life to much growth. A time for great adventures.

185

SIGN	NUMBER	UPPER	MIDDLE	LOWER	LEGEND
	72	B	N	R	Water does not nourish wood. Temper outbursts of temper.
	73	B	N	Y	Relationships reversed. Reexamine, rethink, replan.
	74	B	N	W	Reversed relationships. Abandon desires. Stabilize.
	75	B	N	N	Bridge over heavenly waters. Prospects are positive.

Casting Identification Chart for Upper White

SIGN NUMBER	UPPER	MIDDLE	LOWER	LEGEND
76	W	W	W	Energy of metal strongest. Good fortune.
77	W	W	R	Metal abides fire. Extend patience. Able to act soon.
78	W	W	Y	Power of metal strong. Timely for acting on interest.
79	W	W	B	Excessive use of metal. Use caution engaging help.
80	W	W	N	Much metal generates water. Conditions are ideal.
81	W	R	W	Much metal melted by little fire. Hope not in hopelessness.
82	W	R	R	Metal resists fire. Utilize prosperity. Avoid overambitiousness.
83	W	R	Y	Fire generates earth. Move southwestwardly for gains.

SIGN	NUMBER	UPPER	MIDDLE	LOWER	LEGEND
	84	W	R	B	All powers dormant. Retreat to old places and values.
	85	W	R	N	Elemental relationships are hostile. Loss. Use caution.
	86	W	Y	W	Generating forces maximize. Good spirits now guiding.
	87	W	Y	R	A contrariness of flow. Return to simple elementals.
	88	W	Y	Y	Thick foundations. Rely upon accumulated merit.
	89	W	Y	B	All energies are evenly low. In the late years comfort.
	90	W	Y	N	Everything topsy-turvy. Small people gossip. Meditate.
	91	W	B	W	Wood hacked by metal. Sickness, poverty. Kind helper soon.
	92	W	B	R	Metal masters wood generating fire. Expectancy. Revival.
	93	W	B	Y	Metal cuts wood cracking earth. Dangers abound. Be wary.
	94	W	B	B	Present distress intensifies. Later there is relief.
	95	W	B	N	Damages can be found and repaired. An empty renewal.
	96	W	N	W	Metal generates water abundantly. There can be quick success.
	97	W	N	R	On a seesaw, one is first up then down. Moderation.

SIGN NUMBER	UPPER	MIDDLE	LOWER	LEGEND
98	W	N	Y	Metal yields water resting upon earth. Renew activities.
99	W	N	B	Generating order perfect. Calm clear sailing ahead.
100	W	N	N	Metal produces flourishing water. Great nourishment available.

Casting Identification
Chart for Upper Black

SIGN NUMBER	UPPER	MIDDLE	LOWER	LEGEND
101	N	N	N	Water to the third power. Master of driving forces.
102	N	N	R	Fire extinguished by water. Caution to avoid ruin.
103	N	N	Y	Earth dams water. Great effort to gain reward.
104	N	N	B	Water nourishes wood. Great goals can be secured.
105	N	N	W	Water precedes water. Friendliness founds new strength.
106	N	R	N	Water inundates fire. Disharmonious time. Deep study.
107	N	R	R	Water lessens fire. Great recession. Retrospect, make new plans.
108	N	R	Y	Hidden assets may now be used when times change.

SIGN	NUMBER	UPPER	MIDDLE	LOWER	LEGEND
	109	N	R	B	A time of intermittent confusion. Recovery comes soon.
	110	N	R	W	Negative sequence of overcoming. Gain self-knowledge.
	111	N	Y	N	Excess of water. Great care and skill to survive.
	112	N	Y	R	Elements nonproductive. A hiatus. Study laws of fortune.
	113	N	Y	Y	Water covered by earth. Time of wasted effort. Meditate.
	114	N	Y	B	Overcoming sequence reversed. Persevere in advancing.
	115	N	Y	W	Earth releases water and yields metal. Flourishing time.
	116	N	B	N	Water generates wood two ways. Harness gains. Success.
	117	N	B	R	Yang sequence of generating. Interest determines success.
	118	N	B	Y	Changing sequences make for confusion. Halt. Wait.
	119	N	B	B	Water nourishes wood that abounds. Conditions conducive.
	120	N	B	W	Water feeds wood, metal spares wood. Holding virtue brings success.
	121	N	W	N	Water in abundance. Conditions ideal. Proceed energetically.
	122	N	W	R	Metal giving no water, not melted by fire. Goals by hard work.

SIGN	NUMBER	UPPER	MIDDLE	LOWER	LEGEND
	123	N	W	Y	Unproductive order of elements. Efforts bring illusory rewards.
	124	N	W	B	Changeable sequence of elements. Beware of petty schemes.
	125	N	W	W	Power of metal great. Prospects for gain are immediate.

Bibliography

Bohm, David. *Wholeness and the Implicate Order*. Routledge & Kegan Paul: London, Boston.

Bolen, Jean Shinoda, M.D. *The Tao of Psychology*. Harper & Row: New York.

Capra, Fritjof. *The Tao of Physics*. Shambhala: Berkeley, California.

———. *The Turning Point*. Simon and Schuster: New York.

Chu Hsi and Lu Tsu-Ch'en. *Reflections On Things At Hand*. Columbia University Press: New York.

Dhiegh, Khigh. *The Eleventh Wing*. Nash: Los Angeles.

Eliade, Mircea. *Eranos Yearbooks*. Bollingen Series, Pantheon Books: New York.

Fung Yu-Lan. *History of Chinese Philosophy*. Princeton University Press: Princeton, New Jersey.

Jacobi, Jolande. *Complex/Archetype/Symbol in the Psychology of Jung*. Princeton University Press: Princeton, New Jersey.

Jung, Carl Gustav. *Collected Works*. Bollingen Series, Pantheon Books: New York.

Korzybski, Alfred. *Science and Sanity*. International Non-Aristotelian Library Publishing Company: Lakeville, Connecticut.

Liao, W. K. *Han Fei Tzu: Work from the Chinese*. Arthur Probsthain: London.

Needham, Joseph. *Science and Civilization in China*. Cambridge Publishing: Cambridge, England.

Percival, Harold. *Thinking and Destiny*.

Siu, R. G. H. *The Tao of Science*. M.I.T. Press: Cambridge, Massachusetts.

Strong, James. *Strong's Exhaustive Concordance of the Bible*. Abingdon Press: New York.

Wang Yang Ming. *Instructions for Practical Living*.

Weinberg, Harry L. *Levels of Knowing and Existence*. Institute of General Semantics: Lakeville, Connecticut.

Whitehead, Alfred North. *Modes of Thought*. Free Press: New York.

Whorf, Benjamin Lee. *Language, Thought, and Reality*. Technology Press of M.I.T. and John Wiley & Sons, Inc.: New York.

Wilhelm, Richard. *I Ching or Book of Changes*. Bollingen Series, Pantheon Books: New York.

Wilhelm, Helmut. *Heaven, Earth, and Man in the Book of Changes*. Washington University Press: Seattle, Washington.

Yutang, Lin. *Chinese Dictionary of Modern Usage*. The Chinese University of Hong Kong: Hong Kong.

Zukov, Gary. *The Dancing Wu Li Masters*. William Morrow & Company: New York.